David D Plain

The Plains of

Aamjiwnaang

Our History

To
The Plain family, to whom I belong, especially my father, Nicholas Plain and my uncle
Levi, two grand old men, and all who love aboriginal history

Order this book online at www.trafford.com
or email orders@trafford.com

Most Trafford titles are also available at major online book retailers.

Cover:
Photo image of "Wah-Pus" (The Rabbit, a noted Ahnishenahbi warrior from
Wadiweediwon) by Paul Kane. Painted at Sahgeeng ca. 1845-50. Original
painting is part of the First Peoples Gallery at the ROM, Toronto, Canada.

Printed in the United States of America.

ISBN: 978-1-4251-2273-7 (sc)
ISBN: 978-1-4269-8792-2 (e)

Trafford
PUBLISHING® www.trafford.com
North America & international
toll-free: 1 888 232 4444 (USA & Canada)
fax: 812 355 4082

CONTENTS

12

Preface

In writing The Plains of Aamjiwnaang I have made every effort to capture Aamjiwnaang's early history focusing on one particular family, the Plains. This family claims a long line of chiefs and so they are intrinsically a part of both the community and the Ahnishenahbek Nation's history. We used the word Ahnishenahbek to describe ourselves as a people. Other names we have been known by include Ojibwa and Chippewa. Europeans gave these appellations to us in the early contact period. Ahnishenahbi is the masculine singular and Ahnishenahbikwe the feminine singular of Ahnishenahbek. Today Ahnishenahbek is used in several different ways, to describe our nation or to describe any member of the Three Fires Confederacy and sometimes in an even wider sense to describe any aboriginal people. In this publication I will use it to only describe our Nation or one of our member bands. Concerning grammar, spelling and capitalization I have not endeavoured to correct any errors made in any quotations I have used but left them intact.

Nicholas Plain Jr., my father, was an elected chief of Aamjiwnaang. His father, Ozahshkedawa (On The Plain), was the last traditional chief before the electoral system was imposed upon us under an amendment to the Indian Act in 1884. His father, Misquahwegezhigk (Red Sky) was a chief from Aamjiwnaang. His father, Animikeence (Little Thunder) was both a war chief and a civil chief, as was his father, Kioscance (Young Gull). I will mainly concentrate on these last four generations as their days covered over 200 years from our early dealings with the French through the Indian Act of 1876. Therefore the story moves along very quickly only touching on the main events of a time period or significant episode, which affected or changed the life of the community. I have elected to focus upon this period because the amount of historical data collected includes an era not well appreciated by the general public.

Our story begins with a verbal description of the territory known as Aamjiwnaang but moves very quickly into the different eras of our history, which cascade one upon the other down through time. Each era seems to contain one conflict after another, if not with other First Nations, then with the British or the Americans. Our story follows Kioscance through the Iroquois War and our move to Aamjiwnaang, which was followed by a relatively stable period of trade with both the French and British. The French and Indian War interrupted this golden era and the Beaver War or Pontiac's Rebellion quickly followed. One consequence of Pontiac's resistance to the British was the Royal Proclamation of 1763, which the British colonists hated. It prevented them from expanding westward over the Appalachians and this led to the American Revolution, which we were involved in as allies of the British protecting the frontier. Kioscance's son Animikeence emerges as a war chief during this period.

When the Americans won their independence the British abandoned their First Nation allies and we were left to contend with the Americans alone in The Indian War of 1790-1795. Although we initially had stunning successes against the Americans the war culminated with our loss at the Battle of Fallen Timbers. It took about two decades to recover just in time to become allies again with the British in the War of 1812. It is during this period that Chief Misquahwegezhigk was in his prime.

Animikeence is found in the historical record with various spellings including Animithens and Nemekas. He signed many treaties during the latter part of his life, the last of which commenced the reserve era. This proved to be a long period of missionary and government subjection in which there were continuous and strenuous attempts at assimilation. It is also the period when Ozahshkedawa as a traditional chief fought this subjugation as best he could. Also included here are traditional stories as told to me by my father, Nicholas Plain Jr., such as how Ozahshkedawa received his Ahnishenahbek name and how our family acquired the surname Plain. We basically leave our story at the end of the nineteenth century. However I do bring our history up-to-date in summary fashion in the concluding chapter.

I have spent many hours studying first hand accounts and source documents as well as listening to oral history as told by elders such as my father and my uncle Levi Plain. I was fortunate as a boy to be able to sit at the feet of these two grand old men and listen as they visited on our front porch on Exmouth Street in Sarnia, Ontario. Their personal memories stretched back into the nineteenth century and they related accounts gathered from their mentors whose memories dated back to the beginnings of the reserve era.

I am also indebted to earlier historians who collected such source documents as letters, minutes and papers into volumes. This is especially true of the Wisconsin Historical Society and the Michigan Historical Society. Without their collections it would have been impossible to complete my research. The World Wide Web has opened up a whole new avenue for research, which I also found invaluable. I would especially like to mention the University of Toronto's web site "Early Canadiana", the University of Central Michigan's Clark Historical Library site and the University of Indiana's "Miami Indians Ethnohistory Archives." I sincerely hope this work finds favour in your sight and that it will serve as a source of knowledge of the history of the Ahnishenahbek of Aamjiwnaang.

David D. Plain

Aamjiwnaang First Nation Territory

January 2007.

1

Aamjiwnaang—Place Where Mahnedoog Live in the Water

Aamjiwnaang is an Ahnishenahbek word that has no English equivalent. It is descriptive of a unique characteristic of our territory or hunting grounds. When we first located here there were great rapids at the mouth of the river. Huge rocks were strewn at the entrance of the channel producing many sandbars. Below the rapids the river grew very deep with a strong current. Along the banks of the river there were back currents flowing north back toward the lake. This created many eddies and whirlpools among the choppy waters, which seemed to braid it. It was said that if one looked closely and carefully enough one could catch glimpses of the mahnedoog or spirits just beneath the surface. This is the meaning of the name Aamjiwnaang.

Our territory once covered a large area on both sides of the St. Clair River extending north to Goderich in Ontario and to

White Rock in Michigan. Today the name has been localized to one small reserve at Sarnia, Ontario. The discernable history of this territory starts at the beginning of the 17th century when the Sauk Nation occupied it.

Many Sauk villages were concentrated in the Saginaw River watershed but their hunting territory stretched well into Southern Ontario. They were a very powerful nation with a hostile and antagonist disposition. They were constantly making war upon their neighbours, the Ahnishenahbek to their north, the Potawatomi to their south and the Petun and Otahwah in the southern Georgian Bay region. We realized that as individual nations we could do nothing to make the Sauk stop their antagonistic behaviour toward us so a council was held at Mackinaw Island.

War was determined and the Tionontati (Petun or Tobacco Nation) along with their Otahwah neighbours swept down upon the Sauk at Aamjiwnaang. At the same time the Ahnishenahbek and Potawatomi advanced southward along the western shore of Lake Huron to Saginaw Bay.

When they reached the bay they concealed their canoes in the underbrush and travelled only at night moving stealthily along both sides of the Saginaw River. They came upon a main Sauk town and all but annihilated it. A few escaped to another one of their villages located at what is now Bay City, Michigan. This village suffered the same fate as the main town. A few survivors of this onslaught fled to an island about a quarter of a mile up river where they thought they were safe. However, the river froze over that night and the allies were able to cross over attacking and killing all but twelve women whom we took captive.

They continued up the river as each village succumbed to the allies' furious assaults. They took no more prisoners. When the Ahnishenahbek and Potawatomi arrived at the confluence of the Cass, Shiawassee and Tittabawassee rivers they split up into three parties sending a war party up each river. Village after village fell as they massacred all in their way. The faction that moved up the Shiawassee split again at the mouth of the Flint River.

One of their largest towns was located on the bluffs of the Flint near the present town of Flushing. We assailed it immediately and it suffered the same fate as all the villages before it. Another particularly large town just up the *Tittabawassee* was exterminated and its inhabitants were buried in a mass mound on the riverbank. A third very large town on the Cass, in the bend in the river that is now known as Bridgeport, suffered the same fate as all the others.

A great part of the Sauk Nation was destroyed in this war. The remainder fled to Wisconsin. The only prisoners we kept were the twelve women refugees. A Council of the Three Fires Confederacy was held to determine their fate. The council of elders decided to send them west and by treaty they were put under the protection of the Sioux. This caused considerable dismay among the young men of the nations since they were in favour of torturing them.

The war left a very large territory empty. At first the Saginaw watershed was used a hunting ground by the Ahnishenahbek but hunting parties kept disappearing. Some thought that there were still Sauk warriors lurking in the forests exacting their revenge on unsuspecting hunters. Others thought the spirits of fallen Sauk warriors haunted the territory. Saginaw was avoided for decades and it was only used as a place of exile for Ahnishenabi who committed very serious crimes.

Aamjiwnaang remained the territory of the Tobacco Nation until the mid seventeenth century. At that time the

Haudenosaunee (Five Nations Iroquois) from upstate New York conducted a war of dispersion against the Ouendat (Huron), Tionontati, and Attiouandaron (Neutral) Nations, which succeeded in 1649. Of the survivors of this devastating war about six hundred Christian Huron returned to Quebec with the Jesuit missionaries. The remainder, traditional members of the Huron, Tobacco and Neutral Nations, fled north to seek refuge with the Ahnishenahbek. This group became known as the Wyandotte, a corruption of Ouendat. This war left virtually all of Southern Ontario and South Eastern Michigan uninhabited. At first it was used for hunting and trapping but later the Mohawk and Seneca Nations began to establish towns in Southern Ontario. Aamjiwnaang Territory remained in Seneca hands until the Iroquois War of 1698.

Aamjiwnaang was a beautiful place with a temperate climate and an abundance of fish and game. The first European to come down the St. Clair River was Joliet in 1669 but his records and maps were lost when his canoe overturned just before he reached Montreal. The next spring the French priests Dollier and Gallinée came up the river. Gallinée was also an engineer and his map and notes are the first written records of the region.

In 1679 a Recollet priest named Hennepin travelled up the river with La Salle in the historic ship, "Griffon". Father Hennepin's narrative includes an account of their struggle to get into Lake Huron. It reads as follows:

> The current of that strait is very violent, but not half so much as that of Niagara, and therefore we sailed up with a brisk gale, and got into the strait between the Lake Huron and the Lake St. Claire; this last is very shallow, especially at its mouth. The Lake Huron falls into this of St. Claire by several canals, which are commonly interrupted by sands and rocks. We

sounded all of them and found one at last about one league broad without any sands, its depth being everywhere from three to eight fathoms water. We sailed up that canal, but were forced to drop our anchors near the mouth of the lake for the extraordinary quantity of waters which came down from the upper lake and that of Illinois because of a strong northwest wind had so much augmented the rapidity of the current of this strait that it was as violent as that of Niagara. "The wind- turning southerly, we sailed again, and with the help of twelve men who hauled our ship from the shore, got safely the 23rd of August, into the Lake Huron.[1]

In 1686 Governor Denonville instructed Du Lhut to build a fort in the area of de Troit, the name the French gave to the chain of waters that handled the discharge from Lake Huron to Lake Erie. It means "the strait". Denonville had three reasons for choosing this area. A maintained fort here would prevent entrance by the English to the rich fur country to the north. It would hold the Iroquois in check. And it would better maintain their allies with French goods and religion. He built a small fort named Fort St. Joseph at the entrance of Lake Huron where the St. Clair River was the narrowest. Today the site is located at Pine Grove Park in Port Huron, Michigan. The fort was actively garrisoned by coureurs de bois for military reasons for two years and served as a trading post for another six years before being abandoned.

---

[1] William Jenks, *St. Clair County Michigan Its History and Its* People, vol. 1 (Chicago & New York: The Lewis Publishing Co., 1912), 10-11 available from http://www.hti.umich.edu/m/micounty/ last accessed 18 July 2006. By the upper lake and Illinois F. Hennepin means Lake Superior and Lake Michigan.

In 1701 either Cadillac or someone connected with him at Detroit wrote a very enthusiastic description of the straits between Lakes Huron and Erie. Although it is long and rather wordy it is worth inserting here as it gives some idea of the beauty of Aamjiwnaang in its pristine state.

> Since the trade of war is not that of a writer, I cannot without rashness draw the portrait of a country so worthy of a better pen than mine; but since you have ordered me to give you an account of it, I will do so, telling you that Detroit is, probably, only a canal or a river of moderate breadth, and twenty-five leagues in length, according to my reckoning, lying north-northeast, and south-southwest about the 41st degree (of latitude), through which the sparkling and pellucid waters of Lakes Superior, Michigan and Huron (which are so many seas of sweet water) flow and glide away gently and with a moderate current into Lake Erie, into the Ontario or Frontenac, and go at last to mingle in the River St. Lawrence with those of the ocean. The banks are so many vast meadows, where the freshness of these beautiful streams keeps the grass always green. These same meadows are fringed with long and broad avenues of fruit trees, which have never felt the careful hand of the watchful gardener; and fruit trees, young and old, droop under the weight and multitude of their fruit, and bend their branches towards the fertile soil which has produced them. In this soil so fertile, the ambitious vine which has not yet wept under the knife of the industrious vine-dresser, forms a thick roof with its broad leaves and its heavy clusters over the head of whatever it twines round, which it often stifles by embracing it too closely. Under these

vast avenues you may see assembling in hundreds the shy stag and the timid hind with the bounding roebuck, to pick up eagerly the apples and plums with which the ground is paved. It is there that the careful turkey hen calls back her numerous brood, and leads them to gather the grapes; it is there that their big cocks come to fill their broad and gluttonous crops. The golden pheasant, the quail, the partridge, the woodcock, the teeming turtle-dove, swarm in the woods and cover the open country, intersected and broken by groves of full-grown forest trees, which form a charming prospect, which of itself might sweeten the melancholy tedium of solitude. There the hand of the pitiless mower has never shorn the juicy grass on which bisons of enormous height and size fatten. The woods are of six kinds-walnut trees, white oaks, red, bastard ash, ivy, white wood trees and cottonwood trees. But these same trees are as straight as arrows, without knots, and almost without branches except near the top, and of enormous size and height. It is from thence that the fearless eagle looks steadily at the sun, seeing beneath him enough to glut his formidable claws. The fish there are fed and laved in sparkling and pellucid waters, and are none the less delicious for the bountiful supply (of them). There are such large numbers of swans that the rushes among which they are massed might be taken for lilies. The gabbling goose, the duck, the teal and the bustard are so common there that, in order to satisfy you of it, I will only make use of the expression of one of the savages, of whom I asked before I got there whether there was much game there. 'There is so much,' he told me, 'that it only moves aside (long enough) to allow the boat to pass.' Can it be thought that a land in which nature has distributed everything in so complete a manner could refuse to the hand of a careful husbandman who breaks into its fertile depths the return which is expected of it? "In a word, the climate is temperate, the air very pure; during the day there is a gentle wind, and at night the sky, which is always placid, diffuses sweet and cool influences, which cause us to enjoy the benignity of tranquil sleep.[2]

A traditional story confirms Father Hennepin's description of the mouth of the St. Clair River. It is related that long ago during our forefather's time (probably the early eighteenth century) the most easterly channel of the river ran from Lake Huron through the eastern end of Canatara Park flowing in a southerly direction and empting into the wetlands at Sarnia Bay. Late in November there arose a storm fiercer than anyone could remember. The old ones understood this storm to be caused by a giant thunderbird, which lit on the waters near the mouth of the river. This creature was so huge that its wingspan was several miles wide. It began to thrash in the lake flapping its gigantic wings churning the water into huge waves and creating a terrible wind. This wind howled for several days and was so powerful that it changed the shoreline of the lake blocking off the eastern channel, which diverted the discharge of Lake Huron to the other channels. Lake Chipican in Canatara Park is the only vestige of the eastern channel of the River St. Clair.

---

[2] Ibid., 11-12.

2

Glory Days—Iroquois War: 1698-1701

By the end of the seventeenth century the Ahnishenahbek were located around Lake Superior and along the north shore of Georgian Bay. In particular the Amikouai band or Beaver People lived around the French River, the Oumisagai band or Eagle People inhabited the north shore of Georgian Bay along the Mississauga River and the Nipissing resided inland around a large lake that became their namesake. The Bawitigwakinini band or People of the Falls were located along the southern shore of Lake Superior including both sides of the St. Mary's River. We had moved further west to La Pointe when the Iroquois dispersed the Ouendat but returned to Bawitig (Sault Ste. Marie) about fifteen years later.

The Iroquois had been harassing Ahnishenahbek traders on their way to Quebec by killing them and stealing their pelts. They had been doing this for fifty years. Several peace accords with them had failed. One final peace council was held at the mouth of the Saugeen River and it failed. According to George Copway (Kahgegagahbowh) the Mohawks held the peace for a short time but soon returned to their old ways of waylaying Ahnishenahbek traders on their way to Montreal killing them and stealing their goods.[3] According to a traditional story during the negotiating of this peace accord at Saugeen the Mohawks kidnapped a son of one of the Ahnishenahbek chiefs. They killed him, cooked him and fed him to their guests at the peace feast, including his own father! This occurred around in the fall of 1697. This atrocity was too much to endure and war was determined as the only solution to the "Iroquois problem".

The Three Fires Confederacy and their allies met in council and a strategy was devised to surround the Iroquois by advancing in a pincher movement then attacking simultaneously. The following May each division was to leave Bawitig at the same time. The Bawitigwakinini and their allies the Potawatomi and Wyandotte advanced south to Lake St. Clair and up the Thames River. They were to destroy a large Seneca town, which was located about twelve miles up river. The Oumisagai moved east along the Mattawa River and then south into eastern Ontario while the Amikouai and the Otahwah moved south to the southern shore of Georgian Bay, ready to attack from there.

The major War Chief who led the western division of Ahnishenahbek, Potawatomi and Huron warriors was Kioscance or Young Gull. He was the major chief of the Bawitigwakinini, who as a young man re-located us to the Sault Ste. Marie area from La Pointe. His son, Animikeence, said his

---

[3] For Copway's account of the Iroquois War see G. Copway, *The Traditional History and Characteristics of the Ojibway Nation* (London: Charles Gilpin, 1850), 77-94 available from http://www.canadiana.org/eco/english/index.html last accessed 18 July 2006.

father's fleet of war canoes numbered 400 containing eight warriors each.[4] He first led his forces south to Lake St. Clair where they annihilated the large Seneca town located twelve miles up the Thames River. It was our tradition to desecrate the bodies of their slain enemies by decapitating them and piling their heads into a large pyramid. Our own slain were buried, complete with personal items including weapons, in a mass grave and with full honours. (See the map in Appendix 1 for evidence of this practice.)

Young Gull then moved north along the eastern shore of Lake Huron and assailed the Mohawks at the mouth of the Saugeen River.[5] An historian recording Michigan history writes, "It is related that Kioscance was chief of the Otchipwes in their wars against the Wyandots and Six Nations. In his expedition from Lake Superior to Lake Erie, his fleet was so extensive as to cover the St. Clair River from Fort St. Joseph, or Gratiot, to Walpole Island. On his return from the lower lakes, he camped at Fort Gratiot, and afterward made the district his home."[6]

George Copway wrote in 1850, "Tradition informs us that seven hundred canoes met at Kewetawahonning ... one party was to take the route toward the river St. Clair and meet the southern Hurons ... Those who had gone to St. Clair had likewise a fierce battle at the mouth of a river called by the Algonquin Sahgeeng".[7] This great battle was fought on the flats

---

[4] Peter Schmalz, *The Ojibwa of Southern Ontario* (Toronto: University of Toronto Press, 1991), 23.

[5] Ibid., 22.

[6] History of St. Clair County, Michigan, Illustrated (Chicago: A.T. Andreas Co., 1883), 608 available from http://www.hti.umich.edu/m/micounty/ last accessed 18 July 2006. By the Wyandots it is thought that he meant Huron that had been captured and incorporated into the Iroquois.

[7] Copway, *Traditional History*, 87-88.

at the mouth of the Saugeen River. It became know as the Battle of Skull Mound. The artist Paul Kane visited Saugeen in 1845 to do some sketches. He wrote in his journal the following observance of the remains of the Battle of Skull Mound: "The Indian village of Saugeen, meaning 'the mouth of a river' contains about 200 inhabitants (Ojibbeways). It is the site of a former battleground between the Ojibbeways, as usually pronounced, or Ojibwas, and the Mohawks. Of this, the mounds erected over the slain afford abundant evidence in the protrusion of bones through the surface of the ground".[8]

This was not the first time that the Ahnishenahbek had participated in a military exercise against the Iroquois. The year after Fort St. Joseph had been established Denonville had determined to exterminate the Seneca. Du Lhut was instructed to organise a force of coureurs de bois and Ahnishenahbek allies. He gathered a force of 200 Canadians and 500 Ahnishenahbek at Fort St. Joseph. They then proceeded to meet Denonville and his French army of two thousand men at Irondequoit Bay on the south side of Lake Ontario. As a war chief Young Gull no doubt lead part of the Ahnishenahbek forces. As a war of extermination the venture was a failure. They had only burned three Seneca towns and their surrounding crops when Denonville decided that the Seneca had been "taught a lesson". The Ahnishenahbek left in disgust with the French for "warring on the cornfields". It would be another decade before the Ahnishenahbek and their allies would begin their own war with the Iroquois.

Young Gull and his warriors enjoyed as much success at Saugeen as they did at the Thames. After the Battle of Skull Mound they joined forces with the Amikouai chief White Cloud

[8] Paul Kane, *Wanderings of an Artist Among the Indians of North America* (London: Longman, Brown, Green, Longmans and Roberts, 1859), 3.

and the Otahwah chief Sahgimah. There were many battles fought in the first year of the Iroquois war. The historian Peter Schmalz tells us of some of them:

> According to the oral tradition of the two reserves in the Saugeen area, Cape Croker and Chippewa Hill, there were numerous confrontations in their territory. In the weeks following the Battle of Skull Mound, their tradition indicates that battles occurred inland, along the shore and on the islands of Georgian Bay and Lake Huron in the vicinity of the Saugeen (Bruce) Peninsula. The Iroquois lost in a conflict on the clay banks (in Walkerton), on Indian Hill near the Teeswater River, and at Wadiweediwon (Owen Sound). Three hundred warriors were defeated in an entrenched position on the northwest side of White Cloud Island in Colpoy Bay, the island taking its name from the victorious Ojibwa chief. Moreover, weapons of war have been found a few miles away on Griffith Island and at Cabot's head, where tradition indicates another victory occurred. In the Fishing Islands, north of the mouth of the Saugeen River, Red Bay received its name from the condition of the water after the Mohawk were defeated there. Skull Island in the Georgian Bay was also given its name from the remains of the vanquished. Kahkewaquonaby (Peter Jones) in his History of the Ojibway Indians wrote in 1864: There they fell on a large body of the Naudoways (Iroquois) who had been dancing and feasting for several nights, and were so exhausted as to have sunk into a profound sleep the night on which they were killed. The island is called Pequahkoondebaymenis, that is, Skull Island, from the

number of skulls left on it.[9]

Oral tradition comes from interviews with chiefs, band councillors, and other leading members of the communities of Saugeen and Cape Croker reserves in the period 1968-89. The informants are from the major families on the reserves, including the Joneses, Akiwenzies, Masons, Johnstons, Elliotts, Nadjiwons, Kahgees, and Kewageshigs. Local archaeologist Fritz Knechtel was also most helpful. See also Rose M. MacLeod, The Story of White Cloud, Hay and Griffith Islands (Owen Sound, Ont. 1979), 4; and the Wiarton Echo, 3 August 1883, which indicates that a great battle against the Mohawk was conducted at Cabot's Head. The battle on Indian Hill, Lot 22 Concession 15 of Culross Township, is recorded in Marion McGillivary, ed., All Our Yesterdays: A History of Culross Township, 1854-1984 (Owen Sound, Ont. 1984), 20. Many of these accounts are traditions of the farming community passed on from the early pioneers who received them from the local Indians; see Smith, 'Who are the Mississauga?' 'The Mississauga, Peter Jones and the White Man'; Jones, History, 112. The location of Skull Island is not specifically given by Jones; however, James White in 'Place Names in Georgian Bay,' Ontario Historical Society, Papers and Records 11 (1913): 70, identifies one location as Skull Island where 'a large number of skeletons were found in a pit in the rock on the island.[10]

[9] Schmalz, Ojibwa, 23-24.
[10] Ibid.,272.

These are battles that were fought in South-western Ontario but the Iroquois War was much wider in scope. It was fought in the whole of Southern Ontario as well as up-state New York. Numerous skirmishes occurred along the Mattawa River as attested by human bones found in various places as late as the early twentieth century. Battles were fought at the Otonabee River near Lakefield, the Moira River near Madoc, and Rice Lake. Large Iroquois towns were also destroyed on the Ganaraske River, at the mouths of the Rouge and Humber Rivers as well at Burlington Bay. There was an old trail between Burlington Bay and the Grand River where another town was located about half way. It was destroyed as well.

Two of the major chiefs of the Five Nations approached the Governor of New York at Albany to ask for assistance from their British Allies. They explained to the Governor: "But they [Iroquois] are fully & firmly determined, to hold fast on the Covenant Chain made with the English, & that if the Great King of England will defend them against the Dowagenhaws the Twich Twees & other Nations over whom the French have an Influence & who have murdered several of their People since the Peace, They will have no further Correspondance with the French."[11]

The following is the Governor's answer:

Albany 29 August 1700-

The Earl of Bellomont had a Private Conference with Two of the principal Sachems of each of the 5 Nations

---

[11] Peter Wraxall, *An Abridgement of Indian* Affairs, Harvard Historical Studies, vol. 21, 33-34 reprinted in Ohio Valley-Great Lakes Ethnohistory Archives: Miami Collection 1700-1703 available from http://www.gbl.indiana.edu/archives/menu.html last accessed 10 March 2006.

wherein he told them.

You must needs be sensible that the Dowagenhaws, Twichtwees, Ottowawas & Diondedees and the other Remote Indians are vastly more numerous than you 5 Nations, and that by their continual Warring upon you they will in a few years totally destroy you; I should therefore think it prudent & good Policy in you to try all possible Means to fix a Trade & Correspondance with all those Nations, by which means you would retain them to yourselves, and with my Assistance I am in hopes in a short time they might be brought to be united with us in the Covenant Chain, and then you might be brought to be united with us in the Covenant Chain, and then you might at all times go a hunting into their Country without any sort of hazard which I understand is much the best for Bever hunting.

I wish you would try to bring some of them to speak with me, perhaps I might prevail with them to come & live amongst you and I should think myself obliged to reward you for such a piece of Service...They pray that there may be a good regulation of the Trade & Goods sold Cheap that the Remote Indians may see what Pennyworths there is here which will draw them hither.[12]

As can be seen by his answer the British were in no position to be of any assistance in the war and were really interested more in trade than helping their First Nation allies. As a result the Five Nations were driven from Southern Ontario leaving this huge territory empty, the spoils of war. A general peace was

---

[12] Ibid.,34-35, 37.

arrived at with the signing at Montreal of the Great Peace Treaty of 1701.

Different groups of Ahnishenahbek moved into these new hunting and trapping grounds. Young Gull led the Bawitigwakinini to Aamjiwnaang. He had fallen in love with this territory and his village was established on the Black River. We also established villages on the east side of the St. Clair River and at Swan and Saline Creeks, which flow into the western side of Lake St. Clair.

The French called the Bawitigwakinini band Sauteurs or Saulteux (People of the Falls) from the word Saut meaning falls or rapids and the name moved with the band to Aamjiwnaang. This appellation was natural given to us by the French as the Huron name for us was, "Eskiaeronnon-'people of the Skia,e' ("falls")"[13] and the Dakota appellation "Ra-ra-to-oans (People of the Falls).[14]   It was most likely the Amikouai (Beaver gens) Ahnishenahbek who moved into the territories south of Georgian Bay probably under the leadership of White Cloud one of the principal war chiefs during the Iroquois War. White Cloud Island off the Bruce Peninsula on the Georgian Bay side is named after him because of a great victory he won over the Mohawks there.

After the French and Indian War we began dealing with the British who referred to us and the Amikouai as Chippewa. The Oumisagai (Eagle gens) Ahnishenahbek expanded to the area north of Lake Ontario from the Grand River to the north side of the St. Lawrence. They became known as the Mississauga.

---

[13] Vernon W. Kinietz, *The Indians of the Western Great Lakes 1615-1760* (Ann Arbor: University of Michigan Press, 1940; Ann Arbor Paperback, 1991), 318.
[14] William W. Warren, *History of the Ojibway People* (St. Paul: Minnesota Historical Society Press, vol. 5, 1885; Borealis Books, 1984), 96.

The Ahnishenahbek continued to live a traditional life of hunting, fishing and gathering in their new territories until the land surrenders and reserve period of the nineteenth century.

3

The Golden Age: 1701-1755

The same year the Peace Treaty was signed the French decided to close their post at Michilimackinac and relocate one to de Troit. They did this for two reasons. First, they wanted to slow down the fur trade because there was a glut on the European market and second, they wanted to block the English from trade in the upper lakes. The post Cadillac established was named Fort Pontchartrain but later became the city of Detroit.

Cadillac invited all the Lake Nations to move to de troit to be near the post for trade purposes. Some of the Otahwah and Wyandotte left the Michilimackinac area and established villages around Fort Pontchartrain. The Miami and Potawatomi moved there from the St. Joseph River in Michigan. The Mississauga also established a village just north of the post. All this meant good trading prospects for the First Nations, as long as they could keep from fighting amongst themselves.

The French wanted to corner the fur trade in North

America and Fort Pontchartrain was designed to do this. However, the road to monopoly was rocky and French designs were never fully realized. The Miami were on friendly terms with the English and the Ahnishenahbek negotiated safe passage through Iroquois territory to trade at Albany. The French did all they could to thwart this activity but never really succeeded. This competition drove the price of goods down and the First Nations including the Saulteur prospered.

But things were not always so peaceful because some of the various nations living in such close proximity at Pontchartrain were traditional enemies. In 1706 fighting broke out between the Miami and the Otahwah, right in front of the gates of the French fort. This went on for several months and a French soldier and a Recollet priest were killed. This almost caused a war between the French and the Three Fires Confederacy. Finally the combatants retired from the area and returned to their original homelands.

Then Cadillac invited the Fox Nation to move to Detroit and more than one thousand men, women and children did. They soon caused trouble both with the French and the other nations around the fort. The Otahwah had moved back to Detroit and when Sahgimah, one of their leading war chiefs was called a coward the Otahwah and their allies attacked them. After months of siege in 1712 the Fox fled to the mouth of a small creek on the southwest shore of Lake St. Clair. They made a final stand there but were overwhelmed by the Otahwah chasing them from the south and a large force of Saulteur from Aamjiwnaang and Swan Creek who arrived from the north. The Fox were all but wiped out except for a few warriors who escaped back to their relatives at Green Bay. Young Gull, being a war chief from Aamjiwnaang, was probably involved in this action.[15] The Fox Wars continued until 1737.

Despite all of the troubles the Saulteur Band of Ahnishenahbek prospered. During the first half of the eighteenth century they expanded from their village of Aumichoanwaw on the Black River to Poenegowing on the Flint River and to Nepessing at a small lake near Lapeer Michigan. They also expanded to the east side St. Clair River with villages at the mouth of the Ausable River and at Kettle Point on Lake Huron. The villages at Swan and Saline Creeks at Lake St. Clair expanded north with a village called Wapisiwisibi and to the south with one called Machonce. They also established Seginsiwin on the Huron (Clinton) River and Tonquish north of Detroit. The Swan Creek band also expanded into Ontario with a village on the Thames River. Later this village expanded to Bear Creek (Sydenham River) and Kettle Creek on Lake Erie.

The prosperity of the Golden Age brought on a virtual population explosion. When the Ahnishenahbek first arrived at the beginning of the century they had a population of approximately three thousand. The Spanish undertook a census from St. Louis in 1777 giving a "Summary of the Indian tribes of the Misuri River, who are accustomed to come to receive presents at this post, and the number of their warriors, the name of the principal chief of each tribe; the district where they are located; their distance and direction from this village; in what each one is occupied; the profit or harm that each has been in the past; and the enemies of each one." [16] This census reported:

---

[15] For a detailed account of the troubles at Detroit in 1706 and 1712 see *Wisconsin Historical Society*, vol. 16, 228-242, 267-295 available at http://www.perseus.tufts.edu/ last accessed on 15 Mar 2006.

[16] MS. in General Archives of the Indies. Seville; pressmark, "Papeles procedientes de la Isla de Cuba", WHS, Vol. 17, 358.

The Sotu [Saulteur] Tribe

This tribe is composed of three thousand warriors.
The name of the principal chief of this tribe is
Leturno. They are located three hundred and twenty-
five leagues from this village, and eighty leagues from
the Misisipy on a river formed by two lakes, one called
Lake Huron, and the small Lake Sencler [St. Clair}
which leads to the village of Detroit belonging to
Canada. This tribe being so large and being divided in
various districts, no individual notice can be given of
it, except that the principal chief gives signs of great
affection to the district.[17]

Three thousand warriors would put the population at
around fifteen thousand, an increase of 400% over seven
decades!

Young Gull was personally prolific during the early decades
as well.   He had three sons, Shignebeck, Onsha and
Animikeence. Of these three Animikeence or Little Thunder
became the most renowned. He was born circa 1714 and by
mid-century had become a war chief. He no doubt honed his
military skills during the skirmishes of the Fox War.

In 1728 the Governor of New France received a memoir
from the King regarding the Fox. "His Majesty is persuaded of
the necessity of destroying that Nation, as it cannot keep quiet,
and as it will cause, so long as it exists, both trouble and disorder
in the Upper country"[18]. The French colonials enlisted the aid
of their First Nation allies, which included the Ahnishenahbek

---

[17] Ibid., 368.
[18] Extract of a memoir from the King to the Governor and Intendant of
New France, dated at Versailles, May 14, 1728. NYCD. , ix, pp. 1004,
1005 reprinted in WHS, Vol. 17, 21.

of Aamjiwnaang. This war ended in 1737.

In the 1740's a Huron of Sandusky chief named Nicholas sided with the British and determined war on the French with the intentions of destroying Detroit. The Ahnishenahbek of Aamjiwnaang, or Saulteur of Lake Huron as the French called us, along with the Otahwah and Potawatomi of Detroit supported the commandant there and made life so miserable for the Huron that they pleaded with the Governor to remove them to live with their brothers in Quebec.

Young Gull died circa 1747 at the age of 107. He was buried with great pomp and ceremony at the site of his great victory on the Thames in the side of one of the great Ahnishenahbek burial mounds. A great many people from all over the Great Lakes basin attended the burial rites and this imposing ritual was witnessed by local French fur traders.[19] The death of Young Gull coincided with the ominous clouds on the horizon that would bring an end to the golden age.

---

[19] Schmalz, *Ojibwa*, 23.

4

The Beginning of the End—The French and Indian War

By the mid eighteenth century the dynamics of North America had changed. The British had gained much power due to their colonial policy of encouraging settlement. The French had a policy more attuned with profit from the fur trade and so the British colony on the eastern seaboard had far outperformed the French in terms of population. The British colonials were beginning to flex their muscles by pushing outward against First Nations territories in an ever-increasing hunger for land. The First Nations saw this as just more intrusion. Europe understood this as the beginning of a struggle between England and France for an empire in North America.

Although both England and France were powerful nations, the First Nations really held the balance of power in North America. The two European antagonists each needed First Nation alliances. First Nations power came from ownership of the land and the pelts it supplied the fur trade. Whoever they sided with as allies would have the strength to persevere and at this point in history it was the French. First Nations' weaknesses were linked to over dependence on European goods and technology and their inability to coalesce as unified allies. In the end these two things would be their undoing.

Little Thunder continued honing his military proficiency by fighting the British with such redoubtable characters as Charles Langlade. Langlade was from Michilimackinac, the son of Augustin Langlade a French trader and Domitilde the sister of Nissowaquet a major Ahnishenahbek chief. When going on his exploits for the French against the British he would recruit warriors from various bands along the way, including Aamjiwnaang. Langlade's exploits included defeating and killing Miami war chief Memeskia (Old Britain) at Pickawillany, Ohio in 1752, although the southern Saulteux from the St. Clair region probably did not participate in this battle. Because of the close proximity many had intermarried with the Miami and we would not have wanted to kill our relatives.

However, we did go on to participate in many of the encounters with the British that followed Pickawillany. Robert Dinwiddie, Governor of Virginia, assigned a young Major to reinforce the British presence in the Ohio valley. His name was George Washington and he was only 22 years old. He was to support a small party of woodsmen who had been sent to the forks of the Allegheny and Monongahela Rivers to establish a fort there. But the French moved more quickly sending a superior force who proceeded to oust the colonials, destroy their uncompleted garrison, and replace it with a larger, better one. They named it Fort Duquesne.

Washington arrived in the spring of 1754 only to discover he had been out-manoeuvred. Mingo chief The Half-King informed him that the French had sent out a company of soldiers to scour the countryside and attack and kill any English that they found. In reality the French contingent had a summons to be presented to any English found ordering them to withdraw from French territory under the threat of compulsion. Jumonville de Villiers was only ordered to deliver the summons. Washington had a contingent of 40 soldiers, The Half-King and 12 Mingos with him when he surprised the 33 French soldiers and a few of their First Nation allies. They killed ten, including Villiers, and captured the rest. Reinforcements of 265 Virginia Volunteers and another 100 British Regulars arrived to find Washington had withdrawn to a place called Great Meadows where he had hastily erected a stockade, which he named Fort Necessity.

In the meantime Fort Duquesne had been reinforced and had a garrison of 500 soldiers. The French dispatched Villiers' brother Coulon de Villiers with a large contingency of First Nations from Canada. They included Iroquois from La Preséntation, Hurons, Abenaki, Nipissing, and Algonquin, Otahwah from Detroit and "gens du sauts du lac" or people of the falls from the lake. These would be Saulteux from St. Clair, not from Michilimackinac. As a war chief Little Thunder would no doubt have been with this group from Aamjiwnaang.

Villiers also wrote in his journal that when he arrived at Fort Duquesne he found 500 Frenchmen and eleven 'savages', different from the nations he brought, who were from beyond Belle Riviere.[20] They were about to embark on a mission against the English under Chevalier le Mercier. This was postponed

---

[20] Journal of Louis Coulon de Villiers to Governor General Ange Duquesne de Menneville, September 6, 1754 available from http://www.champlain2004.org/html/11/12_e.html last accessed 15 March 2006.

until a council could be held and Villiers could arrange the terms necessary to include his First Nations in the expedition.

We advanced on Fort Necessity with 400 warriors accompanied by 500 French soldiers. After a day of fighting in a drenching rain Washington surrendered his fort by signing a confession that he had assassinated Jumonville de Villiers. He then retreated back across the Allegheny Mountains.

Later he would dispute the word "assassinated" claiming he did not understand French, the document was illegible so he had to rely on his interpreter, a Dutchman Captain Vanbraam. There were other details of the incident also in dispute. The French claimed that Villiers seeing he was outnumbered showed a white flag and shouted that he only had a paper to deliver. The Virginians denied this. So it was this inexperienced, impertinent young Virginian who, by killing a French officer on a courier mission and then signing a document he couldn't read, started the French and Indian War!

In the summer of 1754 at our defence of Fort Duquesne the Ahnishenahbek were credited for death of Major General Edward Braddock and the utter defeat of his army. He had been sent to the colony from England to especially expel the French from the disputed territory. He was fresh from victories in Europe, was a master tactician, and a stern by-the-book disciplinarian. However, his ego and overconfidence would not allow him to adjust conventional tactics to changing conditions. In short he did not appreciate forest warfare or the tenacity of the Ahnishenahbek. When Benjamin Franklin warned him not to discount the First Nations he replied, "These savages may, indeed, be a formidable enemy to your raw American militia, but upon the King's regular and disciplined troops, sir, it is

28   David D Plain

impossible that they should make an impression."[21]

The British were advancing in a long column on the fort with a vastly superior force. General Braddock commanded fifteen hundred soldiers and thirteen pieces of artillery. George Washington, the young Major of the Virginia Volunteers who we defeated at Fort Necessity the previous year, had temporarily resigned his commission of Lieutenant Colonel to act as Braddock's aide-de-camp. According to Parkman, Washington had two horses shot out from under him in the ensuing encounter and bullets tore his uniform on four separate occasions (a seemingly embellishment designed to romanticize the future American first president). [22]   Henry Gladwin, who would later defend Detroit against Pontiac, was also wounded in the rout. Another young teamster and blacksmith would escape that day by unhitching one of his horses and bolting straight for his father's farm. He would go on later to find fame as the marksman and "Indian fighter" from Kentucky, Daniel Boone.

We had 637 warriors mostly Ahnishenahbek. Langlade came from Michilimackinac and as was his practice would have recruited warriors from Askunessippi (Thames River), Saginaw as well as St. Clair whose war chief was Little Thunder. It is reputed that Pontiac was also with us leading the Otahwah from Detroit. There was also a small contingent of French with us, 72 Marines and 146 Canadians. The Canadians were mostly boys and fled when the conflict began. We met at the Monoghela River and attacked the two thousand yard long column from both sides firing from behind trees, thickets, rocks, fallen logs and gullies. Some of the British regulars

[21] Richard H. Dillon, North *American Indian Wars* (London: Bison Books Ltd., 1994) 36.
[22] Francis Parkman, *Montcalm and Wolfe* (New York: Da Cappo Press Inc., 1995), 128.

claimed they did not see one of their enemies all day. All they saw were powder flashes and puffs of smoke and so that day the British shot a lot of trees. In a little while the column broke, panic set in and the Red Coats began a pell-mell retreat in total disarray. The British losses were staggering. Braddock was killed and the British lost 977 killed or wounded. We lost only twenty-three.[23]

The western First Nations flocked to the side of the French after Montcalm destroyed Fort Oswego so easily and so decisively in 1756. We gathered in huge numbers at Ticonderoga to support Montcalm in his capture of Fort William Henry. Enumerations reported warriors from some forty-one First Nations totalling 1,779 combatants.[24] This of course included Ahnishenahbek. We were allies with the French who had become our major trading partner so we received no soldier's pay. Instead we were paid for the numbers of enemy killed or taken prisoner and by plunder. This was a time-honoured practice, which went a long way in supporting our war effort.

The Marquis de Montcalm was a scholar/soldier so when Fort William Henry capitulated he followed European military etiquette instead of honouring the longstanding arrangement between New France and its First Nation allies. He promised the British a safe conduct back to Fort Edward. They were to be allowed to march out under French guard with the honours of war, which included keeping their unloaded muskets with them as well as all their baggage. The English also took Montcalm's advice and stove their rum-barrels. All this left little plunder and infuriated the Marquis' First Nation allies so we took matters into our own hands.

---

23 Schmalz, *Ojibwa*, 49.
24 Parkman, *Montcalm*, 282-283.

In order to receive the remuneration due, we attacked the long column of British regulars and their colonial militia, whom were being escorted by 300 French regulars. After the debacle caused by Montcalm's lack of understanding of the importance of our rules of engagement we abandoned him in great numbers. We left Lake George proceeding straight to Montreal with our compensation, which included two hundred prisoners.

The governor rebuked us for breaking the capitulation, but the rebuke rang hollow. Colonel Bougainville thought our prisoners of war should have been taken from us and we should have been sent home in disgrace. Instead we were paid the price of two kegs of brandy for each prisoner's release. We were also given guns, canoes and other presents before we left Montreal. The Intendant Bigot was so fearful of our strength that he added in his report "they must be sent home satisfied at all costs".[25] Although the French won the battle at Fort William Henry they also lost the war there. The history books teach that France lost the continent on the Plains of Abraham but that was only a last gasp. Montcalm really lost the continent at Fort William Henry.

---

[25] Ibid., 305.

5

No Longer Essential: 1760-1776

The colonial mentality of Europe allowed for the claiming of new territory by "right of discovery", a principle never understood by First Nations. However, under this principle France had "claimed" a large part of the continent across the middle from the Atlantic to the Mississippi River and south to the Gulf of Mexico. They called this French "possession" New France. New France, of course, included Aamjiwnaang. The British had gained the Atlantic seaboard partly by this outlandish principle and partly from the Dutch. After the French and Indian War the British succeeded as the dominant European power in North America claiming New England and New France as their own.

Not only did we have to contend with this colonial mentality we no longer had two European governments to play against each other. We were no longer, at least for now, needed as military allies. We were subjected to the policies of the new

Commander-in-Chief of the British Forces in America, Sir Jeffery Amherst. His colonial policy regarding First Nations was much different than that of the French.

We had allowed the French to build trading posts on our territory as a convenience to us in our trading activities and we did not understand why the British had to reinforce them with heavier armament after 1760. Who were they arming against?

Amherst's feelings toward the First Nations were well documented in his own writings. Deputy Superintendent of Indian Affairs George Croghan wrote to Amherst in April 1763, "By Letters from Major Gladwin & Capt Campbell at Detroit, which I have received, I understand the Indians in them parts, seem uneasy in their Minds, since they heard so much of North America is Ceded to Great Britain; and the Indian Nations this way seem somewhat Dissatisfied since they heard it, and Says, the French had no Right to give away their Country; as, they Say, they were never Conquered by any Nation; And I am of Opinion the Accounts of the Peace, & hearing so much of this Country being given up to Great Britain, has thrown them into Confusion & prevented their bringing in all our Prisoners this Spring, as they Promised."[26]

Amherst answered, "I am Sorry the Indians should Entertain such Idle Notions regarding the Cessions that have been made by the French Crown; But I Trust they will, on due Consideration, Deliver up all the Prisoners, agreeable to their first Promise, and not Drive us to the Necessity of Using Harsh Methods, when it is in their Power to Secure our Friendship by

---

[26] Crogan George in: B.M., Add. MSS. 21634 f. 235 C. and in Stevens et al., The Papers of Col. Henry Bouquet, Series 21634, 1940, 159 in OVGLEA: MC available from http://www.gbl.indiana.edu/archives/miamis14/miamitoc16.html last accessed 25 March 2006.

Voluntarily Complying with our Request."[27]

He wrote to Colonel Bouquet, "The Post of Fort Pitt, or any of the Others Commanded by Officers, can certainly never be in Danger from such a Wretched Enemy as the Indians are, at this time, if the Garrisons Do their Duty; I am only Sorry, that when such Outrages are Committed, the Guilty should Escape; for I am fully convinced the only true Method of treating those Savages, is to keep them in proper Subjection, & punish, without Exception, the Transgressors."[28] And again, "I Wish there was not an Indian Settlement within a Thousand Miles of our Country; for they are only fit to Live with the Inhabitants of the Woods, being more nearly Allied to the Brute than the Human Creation."[29] Amherst saw us not as sovereign nations but as subjects of Great Britain at best or not even human at worst.

The French had a policy of present giving, which they used to purchase First Nation alliances. We saw it as a sort of rent for the land occupied by their posts and as a toll allowing safe passage through our territories. Amherst looked upon present giving as a policy of bribery. "Service must be rewarded; it has

---

[27] Amherst, Sir Jeffery in: B.M., Add. MSS. 21634 f. 247, L.S. and in Stevens et el. The Papers of Col. Henry Bouquet, Series 21634, 1940, 165 in OVGLEA: MC available from http://www.gbl.indiana.edu/archives/miamis14/miamitoc16.html last accessed 25 March 2006.

[28] Amherst, Sir Jeffery in: B. M., Add. MSS. 21634, f. 271, L. S., and in Series 21634, 182 in OVGLEA: MC available from http://www.gbl.indiana.edu/archives/miamis14/miamitoc16.html last accessed 25 March 2006.

[29] Amherst, Sir Jeffery in: B. M., Add. MSS. 21634, f. 343, L. S. and in Series 21634, 232 in OVGLEA: MC available from http://www.gbl.indiana.edu/archives/miamis14/miamitoc16.html last accessed 25 March 2006.

ever been a maxim with me. But as to purchasing the good behaviour either of Indians or any others, [that] is what I do not understand."[30]

British traders were also harder to deal with than the French had been. The practice of giving credit for goods until after the fall hunt was no longer honoured. This put us in danger of starvation. Amherst responded to our complaints by cutting off the present giving including arms and ammunition, which he said we had in abundance. This claim was untrue and lack of ammunition meant starvation. Amherst's "Indian" policy made the situation all the more fertile for hostilities leading to what we called the Beaver War. The British called it Pontiac's Rebellion or Pontiac's Conspiracy.

The Great War Chief Pontiac summed up the degraded state of our relations with the British in a speech calling the Otahwah, Huron and Potawatomi to war.

> It is important for us, my brothers that we exterminate from our land this nation which only seeks to kill us. You see, as well as I do, that we cannot longer get our supplies as we had them from our brothers, the French. The English sell us the merchandise twice dearer than the French sold them to us, and their wares [are worth] nothing. Hardly have we bought a blanket, or something else to cover us, than we must think of having another of the kind. When we want to start for our winter quarters they will give us no credit, as our brothers, the French, did. When I go to the English chief to tell him that some of our comrades are dead, instead of weeping for the dead, as our brothers, the French, used to do, he makes fun of me

---

[30] Schmalz. *Ojibwa*, 64.

and of you. When I ask him for something for our sick, he refuses, and tells me that he has no need of us. You can well see by that that he seeks our ruin.[31]

Pontiac later sent war belts to many of the western nations as a call to arms. Most of these nations responded and all the western British forts fell but two. These were Fort Pitt and Detroit, which were put under siege. War Chiefs Wasson and Sekahos were called to help with the siege of Detroit. Wasson responded by arriving with two hundred and fifty Ahnishenahbek warriors from Saginaw. Sekahos came with one hundred and twenty warriors from the Thames and Kettle Creek. Later another fifty Mississauga Ahnishenahbek from the Grand River joined him. Interestingly the Ahnishenahbek from St. Clair were not sent a war belt and seemingly did not participate. Schmalz mentions that besides the influential Mississauga chief Wabbicommicot from Toronto "Only one other unnamed Ojibwa chief from Southern Ontario maintained a neutral stand."[32] Could this have been Little Thunder?

In June of 1763 Amherst responded to the upheaval by suggesting to Colonel Bouquet at Fort Pitt "that blankets should be infested with small pox and be given to the Indians as presents". Apparently it was not Bouquet that carried through with the insidious plan but a Captain Simeon Ecuyer who gave the Delaware chiefs two blankets and a handkerchief from the small pox hospital. This was the first attempt at biological

---

[31] "Journal or History of a Conspiracy by the Indians Against the English, and of the Siege of Fort Detroit, by Four Different Nations, Beginning on the 7th of May 1763", Michigan Pioneer Historical Society Collections, Vol. 8, 273-274 available at http://www.perseus.tufts.edu/cgi-bin/ptext?doc=Perseus%3Atext%3A2000.03.0114 last accessed 25 March 2006.
[32] Schmalz, *Ojibwa*, 72.

warfare and it seemed to have had a measure of success. Small pox spread through the First Nation communities in the Ohio valley shortly after the summer of 1763.

This was not the only attempt to gain a distinct advantage over their First Nation allies by unconventional means. Before the Beaver War British traders were prohibited from carrying, selling or giving strong liquor to us. After the Beaver War when peace agreements were in place the British enacted an unofficial policy of unrestricted liquor trade designed to bring the First Nations to their knees. Major Gladwin said "The free sale of rum will destroy them more effectually than fire and sword" and alcohol flowed freely to the First Nations.[33]

The Beaver War lasted in earnest from May through October 1763 and then the confederacy began to fall apart. Hostile French troops from Illinois were expected to help but never arrived. The hostilities did, however, accomplish great things. The British Government recalled General Amherst and softened its "Indian Policy" by adopting a present giving policy similar to the one employed by the French. In order to transform First Nation loyalties from the French to the English they replaced the large French medals the chiefs had in their possession with British ones. More importantly the King issued "The Royal Proclamation of 1763", which legally recognized First Nation land ownership. It is still in force in Canada today and is often used in land claim settlements.

Unfortunately the Proclamation was very hard to enforce. Settlers were anxious to cross the Allegheny Mountains into the Ohio Valley in search of land to homestead. Their intrusions only served to make the Shawanee and Delaware Nations of the Ohio belligerent. The British were now recruiting

---

[33] Ibid., 82.

Ahnishenahbek warriors to help them quell the unrest in Ohio country.

The first implication in the historical record of Little Thunder occurred in the Diary of the Siege of Detroit by Major Robert Rogers. In an entry dated October 8, 1764 he writes, "This morning Mr. Minechesne arrived from Coll. Bradstreet with some Indians, who brought Orders for Mr. Cheppaton to spare no Expense in the Getting some Indians of each Nation to take up the Hatchet against the Shawanys & Delawares & for Minechesne to bring the little Chief of the Chippewas in particular."[34]   Also on two other occasions Rogers mentions "the little Chief" bringing information to the post's interpreter, Mr. Labute. Although "the little Chief" remains unnamed Little Thunder was a chief at this time and his physical stature was small. Judge Z.W. Bunce, the first judge to arrive in St. Clair County, described him in 1817 as being "one hundred and five years old, five and one half feet high".[35]   Many Ahnishenahbi averaged six feet in height.

Although the next decade was relatively quiet relations between the First Nations and the British were strained. The British colonials hated the Proclamation of 1763 because it attempted to prohibit expansion westward. They all but ignored it and settlers poured over the Allegheny Mountains into "Indian Territory". This caused much turmoil and at first, when things got out of hand, the British colonial government tended to leave "Indian Custom" to settle matters instead of British law. Then they shifted their policy to using British Law but they

---

[34] Rogers, Major Robert. *Diary of the Siege of Detroit*, unfinished, 111 available from
http://www.canadiana.org/ECO/ItemRecord/64039?id=c2c3384897058bda last viewed 25 March 2006.
[35] *History of St. Clair County*, A.T. Andreas, 608.

applied it unevenly.

In 1767 George Croghan made a trip from New York to Detroit and back to ascertain the state of "Indian affairs" in the newly acquired territories. On the way to Detroit he heard from several First Nation sources that a large council involving some twelve nations was to meet the following spring but he could not ascertain the purpose of such a council. However, he was given a sample of the complaints the First Nations were levelling at the British. The following is from Croghan's journal of that trip:

> [October] 27th: Came to a large hunting Village of the Delawares, where I met some Chiefs and Warriors of that Nation, who pressed me to stay with them that and the day following, which I agreed to.

> [October] 28th: In the Morning We met at a fire prepared by the Indians for that purpose. I informed them that I was going to Detroit to restore their Friends the Two Chippawas that had been sent Prisoners to Albany. They Answered, that they were glad to hear it, as the Nations over the Lakes were making a great complaint to their Allies- that every little Crime which any of their People committed in their drink- was taken great Notice of by the English at the same time refused to punish their Negroes for Murdering their People before their faces, and that they were not able to obtain Justice from the English for any injuries they did them. The Delawares reply'd We know this to be true; we could never obtain Justice from you, when any of our People were Murdered by Yours; When at the same time, if any of our People took a Horse from Yours, you always followed us, and

insisted for Satisfaction. They then said, We do not mention this in Anger, tho' We have suffered, only to let you know, that we are sensible when we are ill treated, and do not forget the injuries done us.

In Answer to this, I used every Argument in my Power to convince them, That every step that was in the Power of the General, and Superintendent; were taken to bring such People as committed Offences in the Indian Country, to Justice. To Which they Answered, "We thought you had Laws for that purpose." [36]

Crogan went on to Detroit where he had several meetings with various chiefs from the Nations living around that post. He still could not establish the purpose for the grand council called for in the spring. However, he did have other grievances to redress so he called a general council with the chiefs of all the First Nations living in the Detroit area. The first day he laid out his complaints to the chiefs, which mostly dealt with violence toward British settlers. The following day they reconvened and the "Chief of the Chippewas" answered the Deputy Superintendent's complaints acting as speaker for the assembly:

Father, We have considered of the Several Speeches You made us Yesterday; Every thing You Said to Us is truth, We cannot deny but our Conduct has been very bad. We have lost some of our People by the English which You know as well as ourselves; You have now brought Two of our People of Life, and given them to

---

[36] Croghan, George in: Peckham, *Croghan's Journal . . . 1767*, 33-34, 43-44 in OVGLEA: MC available from http://www.gbl.indiana.edu/archives/miamis17/M66-67_32a.html last accessed 27 March 2006.

us, which I hope will learn us to behave better for the future. I Speak to you in behalf of all the Indians present, a great many of our People are out Hunting; I will Call a Council, of all our Nations in the Spring and lay before them you Several Speeches; And You may be assured You shall then have our answer to them, as I am Convinced in my own Heart, that we have behaved ill; I will Speak my Sentiments at that Council, and hope our future Conduct will merit the Approbation of Our Father, as well as our Brethren the Hurons has done: He then gave a Belt.[37]

Then the chief put a complaint to Croghan, "The Same Speaker then Spoke on another Belt and Said Father, when the French had this Country, they always kept a Doctor to attend our Sick People at this Place, and for some time after You came here, You did the Same; We are now, and have been this Summer past very Sickly for want of a Doctor to attend us as formerly, We have lost a number of People, We there fore beg You'll let us have a Doctor to attend us when Sick."[38] This Chippewa Chief remains unnamed but probably was Little Thunder since Sekahos had gone to the Illinois with Pontiac and then had returned to his territory on the Thames. Wasson had returned to Saginaw after the war. Both had made submissive speeches to the British begging forgiveness for their parts in the war and had gone off to lick their wounds.

Croghan left Detroit arriving at Fort Pitt on December 9th. On December 15th finally one of the Delaware chiefs satisfied his curiosity:

[December] 15th: At 10 o'Clock We met in Council,

---

[37] Ibid.
[38] Ibid, 45,46.

when the Indians went thro' the Ceremony of
Condoling with Capt Edmonstone & myself; And
then taking the Belt I had given him Said, Father, You
have been informed by Some of our People, as You
was on your Journey from here to Detroit, who are
now present, of a private meeting we had with Some
of the Six Nations last Summer, & of the Messages
Sent us by the Chippawas, which must Convince You
this Council is not called by us. There has happened
Several little differences between the warriors of our
different Nations during the last war, all which is
intended to be Settled at this meeting; And it is further
proposed to unite the Northern & Western Indians so
that we become One People, & to renew & Strengthen
our antient Friendship with each other which has been
neglected for Some Years Past, this is the true
intention of this meeting; But at the Same time the Six
Nations are to lay before the Council a Complaint
against the English for making Settlements in their
Country before they have been Paid for their Lands;
Have killed & wounded Several of their Warriors last
Year, as they were Passing & repassing to & from war
against the Southern Indians. All which we know to be
true, they seem determined upon having Revenge, and
have told our nations, that as we are part of their
Confederacy, it concerns us as much as them. That the
Country belongs to us all in common, & that they
Expect we will assist them in obtaining Justice from
the English. The speaker then returned me the Belt,
and told me, they had acquainted me with all they

knew concerning the Meeting.[39]

Although most of the turmoil was occurring south of Lake Erie it only served an ominous cloud on the horizon for the Ahnishenahbek. In the meantime we kept living the traditional life rotating throughout Aamjiwnaang territory from the hunting camps to the sugar camps to the fishing camps to summer in the main villages.

However, Little Thunder busied himself in another way. Captain Patrick Sinclair of the 15th Regiment of the British Army was put in charge of transporting supplies between Detroit and Michilimackinac. While acting in this capacity he obtained a deed in 1765 from the Ahnishenahbek for a tract of land on the St. Clair River at the Mouth of the Pine River (present day St. Clair, Michigan). The St. Clair River at first was called the Sinclair River but later the name fell into line with Lake St. Clair, as it had been known for decades.

The tract contained 3,789 acres and included some of the finest stands of white pine in the area. He built a post on the tract, which he named Fort Sinclair and he became the commandant. He also built a mill about four miles up the Pine to produce lumber, which was shipped to Detroit. This area became known as the Pinery. Sinclair returned to England in 1768 where his military career blossomed. He came back to America in 1775 where he was appointed lieutenant governor of Mackinac. His holdings on the St. Clair prospered until after the revolutionary war when they fell into disrepair. When the new boundary was drawn and the property became part of American soil it was sold. Sinclair returned to England in 1784 finally reaching the rank of major general, which he held until his death in 1820.

---

[39] Ibid..

When Sinclair established his fort in 1764 he struck up a friendship with Little Thunder and enlisted him to garrison the fort, which he did in the early days of the post. Little Thunder received from the British the dress and uniform of a brigadier general for his service acting as a soldier under the command of Captain Sinclair.[40] During this period Little Thunder also had two sons, Anchau and Misquahwegezhigk or Red Sky.

---

[40] Jenks, *St. Clair County*, 48.

6

Needed Again—The American Revolution

The American Revolution began in 1775 and at first both sides were decidedly against encouraging First Nation allies to get involved. But after the war dragged on indecisively for two years both began to turn to their First Nation allies for assistance. In the spring of 1777 Charles Langlade began to gather warriors for the British from Superior country at La Baye for an expedition south. From there they were sent to Niagara and held in check until needed. Some twenty-three hundred warriors wintered there awaiting orders. At Detroit the British began to ply them with liquor in order to buy their alliance.[41] However, many were unenthusiastic regarding the war. Some

---

[41] *Haldimand Papers: Capt. R.B. Lernoult to Lieut. Col. Mason Bolton,* in MPHSC, vol. 19, 440. Of the 8750 gallons requested by Captain Lernoult for the first six months of 1778 8250 were allocated for the "Indians"..

were even happy to see the whites fighting amongst themselves. The rebels were looked upon as disobedient children and many felt their chastisement should be left to their father.

It became more urgent for the British to protect the frontier so they began to draw even more First Nation warriors into the conflict. A Council was held at Detroit on June 14th 1778 between the British and "the Ottawas, Chippoweys, Hurons, Pouteonatamiess, Delawares, Shawanese, Miamis, Mingoes, Mohawks & the Tribes of Ouashtanon, Saguinan &c. Delawares Sencas". In total there were sixteen hundred and eighty-three First Nation people congregated there and the council lasted seven days. Both our war chiefs and our village chiefs represented each nation at the council proper. Little Thunder (A-ni-mi-kai-nee) headed the list of nine war chiefs representing the "Chippoweys". He must have been an impressive sight in his headdress, brigadier's coat and large King George III medal hanging around his neck. This is the first recording of his name found in the historical record.[42]

The purpose of the council was to liberally hand out "presents" designed to encourage a commitment by the chiefs to support the war effort. Lieutenant-Governor Henry Hamilton spoke to the council on the first day thanking the conferees for alliances struck the previous year and coming to renew those bonds at this council. The following day Simon Girty was introduced as an interpreter "having escaped from the Virginians and put himself under the protection of His Majesty, after giving satisfactory assurances of his fidelity". Girty was a loyalist who was despised by the revolutionaries who looked upon him as a renegade. One man's partisan is another man's traitor.

---

[42] *Haldimand Papers: Lieut. Gov. Hamilton to Gen. Carlton* in MPHSC, Vol. 9, 442.

Hamilton congratulated us during the council with the following comments:

> You may remember when you received a large belt of alliance here last year, the number of nations who took hold of it, you know the consequences have been good, as you have succeeded in almost all your enterprizes, having taken a number of prisoners and a far greater number of scalps.
>
> You have driven the Rebels to a great distance from your hunting grounds & far from suffering them to take possession of your lands, you have forced them from the Frontiers to the Coast where they have fallen into the hands of the King's Troops, as I had foretold you would be the case, for which good service I thank you in the name of the King my master.[43]

Chamintawáa, a village chief of the Otahwah, spoke on behalf of the Three Fires Confederacy renewing their military alliance with the Crown and promising to continue to ignore poor advice saying, "bad birds come about us and whisper in our ears, that we should not listen to you, we shall always be attentive to what you say".

Some of the Delaware from the Ohio valley had been sympathetic with the rebels and had hindered our efforts to repel them. Chamintawaa took them to task with the following speech:

> Listen Brethren! I am going to say a few words to our Grandfathers the Delawares in the name of all the Nations here present, I speak in the name of their War Chiefs.

---

[43] Ibid., 445.

I speak in the name of our War Chiefs, because in their path they have sometimes found Branches or Stumps laid across, which they desire to know the reason of.

Brethren! we see you, tho' you be far distant, and we observe you breaking down the branches from the trees to lay across our road, at the same hanging down your heads and with tears in your eyes.

Six strings black and white Wampum.

Brethren! we speak to you now in presence of our father, we are not like you, we speak from the bottom of our hearts and want to know why the Path of the Warriors going against the Rebels has been blocked up. We believe you to be the authors of it, this is the opinion of all the War Chiefs, you now see round our father.

We speak to you, because when our Warriors went your way, they were obliged to go out of the road and thereby have suffer'd and return'd with tears in their eyes.--We speak once more to you who came here in fear & trembling.

We address you as well as in the name of the village as the War Chiefs, and desire if you have anything bad in your hearts, that you will leave it here & not carry it away with you, we know you sometimes take your hearts to the Virginians, but we beg you will now leave them here, where ours are all assembled, we beg you to have sense and listen to our father as we all do & obey his will.--These are the sentiments of all here present & this is the last time we intend speaking to you.[44]

The other speakers echoed Chamintawáa but the Delaware did not respond until the end of the conference. Captain James of the Delaware said he could only speak for his village, about sixty warriors, and not his rest of his nation, but he claimed to be wholeheartedly onside and to prove his sincerity he "sang the War Song and danced the War Dance" on the belt he was given. In all fairness to Captain James it was not him that betrayed the First Nations Confederacy but three other Delaware chiefs, Captain Pipe, Captain White Eyes and John Kill Buck, Jr. In September of that year they would sign a treaty with the revolutionary government at Fort Pitt.

The following year there was a turn of events that set back the British's efforts to use their First Nations allies to protect the frontier. The British had been much more successful than the rebels at invoking First Nations assistance in their war effort. The Six Nations of upstate New York were divided. Only the Oneida and Onondaga had faith in the rebel cause and even they were split. Although the revolutionary government had less First Nations onside they were much more adept at the use of propaganda as a instrument of war.

In July of 1778 the British led an expedition of five hundred into the Wyoming Valley to evict six thousand illegal pioneer squatters. Of the five hundred combatants two hundred were members of Colonel John Butler's Rangers and three hundred were First Nations warriors. The First Nations contingent consisted of some Ahnishenahbek but most of them were Seneca. The valley was situated in the midst of the best Seneca hunting grounds, land that was never ceded or sold. The squatters had falsely imprisoned a peaceful hunting party of

---

[44] Ibid.,448-449.

Seneca then proceeded to murder them scalping two men and one woman.

There were several small forts in the valley and they surrendered almost immediately. However, Fort Forty held out and after Butler's warriors feigned withdrawal the rebel force foolishly came out after them, resulting in the killing of 227 rebels. The Congress Party responded to the defeat by releasing outlandish propaganda. One story of the day read the massacre was a 'mere marauding, cruel and murderous invasion of a peaceful settlement . . . the inhabitants, men, women, and children were "indiscriminately butchered" by the 1,100 men, 900 being their Indian allies.'[45] In actuality the force consisted of 500 combatants, 200 British Rangers and 300 First Nation warriors.

A comprehensive study of the accounts done by Egerton Ryerson convinced him that only rebel soldiers were killed and the misinformation put out by the Congress Party was wholly exaggerated and totally inflammatory. It was designed to inflame hatred among the populace against the British and their allies but it had the effect of stirring up hatred for all First Nations.[46] This along with other propaganda releases about indiscriminate killings, torture and scalping convinced General Washington to act.

In 1779 he determined a war of extermination upon the whole of the Six Nations and sent General John Sullivan with six thousand five hundred men to invade Iroquois lands. They were unsuccessful at the task of extermination but the expedition resulted in the total destruction of 40 Seneca and

---

[45] Schmalz, *Ojibwa*, 98.
[46] Ibid., n 20, 283. This note recommends the reader to see Egerton Ryerson, *The Loyalists of American and Their Times: From 1670 to 1816* (Toronto 1880), 2: 85-122 for his findings.

Cayuga towns and all their surrounding crops. The famished Iroquois fled to Niagara putting a tremendous strain on British war supplies. This campaign effectively put them out of action for the duration of the war. The committing of atrocities was not all one sided either. Sullivan's men revelled in the victory by scalping dead Iroquois and in one instance even skinning a corpse from the hips down to make a pair of leggings. Although Sullivan carried out the expedition it gained Washington the nickname of "Town Destroyer".

On the frontier, west of Detroit in Illinois country, George Rogers Clark set out from Kaskaskia to retake Fort Sackville at Vincennes. He had taken it the previous year only to lose it to Colonel Hamilton who had marched immediately to Vincennes from Detroit. Clark embarked on a most arduous military march leaving the 5th February 1779 with some 170 rebels and Frenchmen. His militiamen marched over 150 miles through flooded plains waist deep in freezing water taking Vincennes on the 23rd February. The march was described as "one of the most daring and fatiguing marches in America's military history". He is said to have "scared off Hamilton's Indians by using the old dodge of marching and countermarching his men ... in a patch of prairie visible to the fort, to suggest that he had a larger force".[47] But the Ahnishenahbek had proven time and again that they knew how to equalize a superior force with forest warfare. Besides, a show of force was never known to "scare us off".

The actual reason the alliance pulled back and left Fort Sackville to be taken can be found in a letter from Captain Alexander McKee to Captain R.B. Lernoult. In the correspondence he is quite concerned over news he had

---

[47] Dillon, *North American Indian Wars*, 54.

received from the Three Fires Confederacy:

> I send you the enclosed string of Wampum, it was delivered here by the Otawas in the name of An'qu'shey'ray & it is to inform them that the Ottawas Chippewas and those of their confederacy had entered into a new league of friendship with their ancient Father the French and their Brethren the Virginians therefore that they were determined to interfere no longer, in the quarrel between the white people, it was true they say some of their warriors had been foolish enough to take hold of the hatchet, handed about to the Indians at Detroit, but that their eyes were more opened, and from recovering their senses find they have been deceived both by their fathers the English and the six nations, who have acted with them in the same manner, by putting a hatchet into their hands which if they used any longer must be directed against their old Fathers the French, who they saw were coming Hand in hand with the Virginians. That they were now determined to set still and advised the Shawanese to be wise to do the same as their Brethran. The Wabash Indians have all come into this resolution.[48]

The French, not unlike the First Nations, were fighting on both sides of the Revolution. This was bad news indeed and even though it left the Delaware, Miami and Shawanee as active allies it was still very detrimental to Britain's efforts in quelling the rebellion. Old loyalties die hard. The decision by the Three Fires Confederacy effectively took them out of the war, which

---

[48] *Haldimand Papers: Capt. Alexander McKee to Captain R.B. Lernoult* in MPHSC, Vol. 19, 423.

was quickly followed by the complete route of the Iroquois that summer.   It would be another three years before the Ahnishenahbek of Aamjiwnaang would participate in the "white man's quarrel".

The caldron of hatred toward the First Nations by the dissidents continued to boil. In the spring of 1782 the Moravian Delaware were busily preparing to flee westward from their homes near their town of Gnadenhutten on the Muskingum River, which had become a dangerous war zone. They had been planning to seek safe haven among the Hurons of Sandusky just as their Delaware brothers who were not Moravian Christians had done before them.

These Delaware had long been converted to Christianity by Moravian missionaries and were living in this locale under the auspices of the Moravians. Missionaries led their community; their dress was European as well as their cropped hair. They were pacifists who remained neutral sitting out the war in peace.

Colonel David Williamson and 160 of his militia approached them, apparently peacefully. They promised the Christian Delaware that they were there to give them protection and to remove them to Fort Pitt where they could wait out the war in peace. The Moravians encouraged their brothers to come in from the fields around Salem and take advantage of the militia's good offer. They did and the rebels immediately relieved all of them of their guns and knives, which they promised to return to them later. The rebel's devious lies lulled them into a sense of false security so they put their faith in the seemingly genuine concern of their benefactors. They discovered too late the treachery of the militia. As soon as they were defenceless they were bound and imprisoned charged with being "warriors, murderers, enemies and thieves" because they had in their possession all the implements and goods normally used by white pioneers. The missionaries, of course, had purchased these for them. After a night of praying 29 men, 27 women and 34 children were brutally murdered. Even pleas in excellent English by Christians on bended knees failed to prevent the massacre. Only two escaped by feigning death and they fled to Detroit where their story incensed the Ahnishenahbek.

Fresh off the easy success of this massacre the rebels decided to move deeper into "Indian Country" and annihilate the First Nations at Sandusky. The Wyandotte located there had been especially troublesome. General Irvine of the rebel forces was in favour of such an expedition but declined to appoint its leadership to Colonel Williamson. He abhorred the actions taken at Gnadenhutten under Williamson's leadership. Instead Colonel William Crawford was chosen to lead an expeditionary force of 478 men. They assembled at Mingo Bottoms on the west side of the Ohio River. They were in all secrecy and stealth to make their way westward to where they hoped to take the First Nation towns of Sandusky by surprise. They left Mingo Bottoms on the 25th of May and instead of taking the established "Williamson Trail" they moved in a series of forced marches through the wilderness.

The expedition passed unknowingly very close to the camp of Delaware chief Wingenud then crossed the Little Sandusky where on June 4th their objective came into view. They had travelled ten days and the only signs of hostile forces they saw were two scouts on the third day, which they chased off. They believed their covert operation had been a success.

What they didn't realize was that we had known their ambitions from the beginning. The long advancing column had been shadowed the whole time and reports of their progress passed along to the chiefs daily. War belts were sent to neighbouring Wyandotte, Delaware and Shawanee towns to assemble at the Half King, Pomoacan's village. Major Arent S. De Peyster commandant of Detroit was sent an urgent call for help. He responded by dispatching Captain William Caldwell with 70 Rangers, 44 "lake Indians" and 150 Wyandotte. Alexander McKee's 140 Shawanee reinforced them. All were converging on the unsuspecting rebels at Sandusky.

Crawford and his company of revolutionaries were dumbfounded for upon reaching their objective they found the town completely deserted. It had been abandoned some time before when the inhabitants realized its location was precarious. The rebel force became confused and so its officers held a council and decided to move up river in hopes of still surprising the Wyandotte. They soon met a force from Pemoacan's town and were held at bay until Shawanee, Delaware and the force from Detroit arrived, which they soon did. The ensuing battle lasted from June 4th to the 6th and ended with a complete First Nations' victory. Their expedition to destroy the First Nation towns of Sandusky ended in disaster costing the Virginians 250 killed or wounded. The British suffered two killed and two wounded and the First Nations suffered four killed and eight wounded. Williamson, the leader of the Moravian massacre, was able to lead the rebel survivors back to safety. However, Crawford was captured along with some of the other perpetrators and taken to a Delaware village where they paid for Williamson's atrocities with their lives.

One of the names the British had for the Ahnishenahbek of Aamjiwnaang was "lake Indians". The fact that they only supplied the expedition from Detroit with 44 warriors attests to their resolve to remain neutral. They were probably some of the young men incensed by the news from Gnadenhutten. If any war chiefs were involved they would no doubt have raised a much larger force. The British were disappointed in the lack of enthusiasm for their cause. Caldwell complained in a letter to De Peyster that "The Lake Indians are very tardy, we had but Forty-four of them in action".[49]

One of the last excursions the Ahnishenahbek of Aamjiwnaang participated in became known as the Battle of Blue Licks. Captain Alexander McKee was one of the British's most successful agents at raising a body of First Nation warriors. In August of 1782 he had raised 300 Huron and "lake Indians" for an expedition into Kentucky. After an unsuccessful siege of a settlement called Bryant's Station the warriors retreated to a piece of high ground at the Blue Licks, on the middle fork of the Licking River. They waited there to ambush the enemy who were in pursuit with a force of 200 picked men. The warriors totally defeated them. They suffered 140 killed or wounded. McKee's forces had 10 killed and 14 wounded. They only gained 100 rifles as some of them were thrown into a deep part of the river and not recovered. The rebel enemy were commanded by Colonels Todd, Trigg and Boone along with Majors Harlin and McGeary most of whom fell in battle. The rest escaped in a pell-mell retreat back to their settlement. Colonel Boone was the same Daniel Boone that fled the rout and death of General Braddock in 1755.

The Treaty of Paris in 1783 ended the conflict. The Continental Army emerged victorious and a new nation was born. The name of this new nation was the United States of American and its citizens came to be called Americans. The Ahnishenahbek called them Gchi-mookmaan or Big Knives after the sabres their soldiers carried at their sides. Gchi-mookmaan soon became a derogatory term due to the treatment First Nations received from the Americans.

---

[49] *Haldimand Papers: Capt. William Caldwell to Major Arent S. De Peyster* in MPHSC, Vol. 20, 25.

Although the British were the apparent losers in the
American Revolution the real losers were the First Nations.
This was especially true of the Iroquois. Land that was not
Britain's to surrender was given up. This land belonged to the
Six Nations and they complained bitterly. In a council with
Brigadier General Allen McLean at Niagara Principle Chief
Captain Aron protested:

> ...they never could believe that our King could
> pretend to cede to America what was not his own to
> give, or that the Americans would accept from him
> what he had no right to grant. That upon a
> representation from the Six Nations in the year 1768,
> the King had appointed Sir William Johnson as
> Commissioner to settle the boundaries between the
> Indians and the Colonies, That a line had been drawn
> from the Head of Canada Creek (near Fort Stanwix) to
> the Ohio, that the boundaries then settled were
> agreeable to the Indians and the Colonies, and never
> had been doubted or disputed since--That the Indians
> were a free People subject to no power upon earth--
> That they were the faithful Allies of the King of
> England, but not his subjects, that he had no right
> whatever to grant away to the States of America, their
> right or properties without a manifest breach of all
> Justice and Equity, and they would not submit to it.[50]

McLean responded in his report to General Frederick
Haldimand, Governor of Quebec, "I do from my soul Pity these
People" for "the miserable situation in which we have left these

---

[50] *Haldimand Papers: Brig. Gen. Allan McLean to Gen. Frederick Haldimand* in
MPHSC, vol. 20, 118-119.

unfortunate People".[51] The British were also worried about the reaction of all the Western Nations as they began to abandon their posts. With this new entity to contend with things only became worse for First Nations people. Even though treaties with First Nations had to be ratified by Congress, like treaties with other sovereign nations, American policy would abandon the concept that First Nations were sovereign or that they were even nations at all.

Three years later in a speech to the Congress of the United States many First Nations expressed their dissatisfaction with their treatment by the U.S. following the conclusion of the American Revolution. In 1784 the British Colonial government purchased land in Southern Ontario from the Mississauga for the displaced Six Nations to settle on. Six hundred and seventy-five thousand acres for the followers of chief Joseph Brant, the whole length of the Grand River six miles deep on each side, and another large tract in the Bay of Quinte area for the followers of Mohawk chief John Deserontyon. At the same time a flood of United Empire Loyalists began to relocate from the U.S. to Ontario, a migration that would change the lifestyle of the Ahnishenahbek forever.

---

[51] Ibid.,121.

7

Betrayal—The Indian War of 1790-1795

The border determining lands ceded to the Americans with "Indian Country" continued to be a major stumbling block to peace between the First Nations and the United States of America. First Nations insisted the boundary line agreed upon in the Treaty of Fort Stanwix in 1768 be adhered to. That boundary line was the Ohio River. However the American government's official policy was not to discuss any boundary line but instead to offer to compensate the First Nations with goods and annuities for huge tracts of land to be opened up for white settlement. Huge numbers of American pioneers had already crossed the Ohio to squat on First Nations territory even under the threat of attack and certain death.

In fact the Big Knives claimed all the territory south of the Great Lakes as far west as the Mississippi as theirs according to the 1783 Treaty of Paris. In 1785 Congress passed an

Ordinance to divide the territory north and west of the Ohio into states to be governed as a territory. In 1787 they passed a more complete Ordinance appointing Major General Arthur St. Clair Governor of the new Northwest Territory. This huge tract of land encompassed what is now the States of Ohio, Michigan, Indiana, Illinois and Wisconsin.

The Miami War Chief, Little Turtle had forged a confederacy that included the war chiefs and warriors of the Miami, Potawatomi, Shawanee and Ahnishenahbek. Little Thunder, was the pre-eminent war chief of the Ahnishenahbek and his two sons; Red Sky and Anchau were young warriors at this time. The many skirmishes that ensued during the late 1780's led to decisions by Washington that would at first prove disastrous to the Big Knives.

In 1790 President George Washington authorized Governor St. Clair to raise troops to punish our Confederacy for having the audacity to defend our lands. To this end he raised a force of twelve hundred militia and 320 regulars at Fort Washington, Cincinnati, to be led by Brigadier General Josiah Harmar. Little Turtle and his confederacy retreated before Harmar's lumbering army. They lured Harmar deeper into their territory where they had set at trap in the Maumee Valley near what is now Fort Wayne, Indiana. After stringing out his army into one long column Little Turtle sprung the trap attacking the column's flank killing 183 and wounding 31. Harmar's army was panic stricken and fled in disarray. Harmar claimed a victory but had to face a board of inquiry where his defeat was whitewashed. However, none other than Major General St. Clair would replace him.

In 1791 St. Clair raised an army of fourteen hundred militia and six hundred regulars and he marched them out of Fort Washington to finish what Harmar had failed to do. St. Clair established two weak outposts named Fort Hamilton and Fort Jefferson and then chose as his base a high spot on the Wabash about fifty miles from present day Fort Wayne. By this time his army had shrunk to fourteen hundred due to desertions. Little Turtle's alliance attacked the army's camp head on at dawn scattering the Kentucky militia. St. Clair tried to rally his troops but to no avail. His second in command, General Richard Butler lay wounded on the battlefield. The militia shooting wildly hit some of their own men and bayonet charges were mowed down with gunfire from the surrounding forest.

St. Clair lost half his army while standing his ground but when he realized he was threatened with total annihilation he ordered a retreat, which was no orderly one. Most of his men threw away their arms in a panic stricken flight. With close to one thousand casualties this would be the worst defeat the United States would ever suffer at the hands of the First Nations. The incident on the Wabash became known as "St. Clair's Shame". President Washington cursed St. Clair for being 'worse than a murderer'.[52] First Nations' hopes and confidence soared.

Runners were dispatched to all nations from Alabama to the Great Lakes as far west as the Mississippi to invite them to smoke the pipe in support of the united defence of their land and country. In October 1792 the Shawanee hosted a great congress at the Glaize, where the Auglaize River flowed into the Maumee. Delegates from a wide range attended: Shawanee, Delaware, Mingos, Miami, Munsees, Cherokees and Nanticoke whose territories needed defending. Also present and promising support were Wea from the Wabash, Sacs and Fox from the Mississippi, Six Nations and Mahicans from New York and

---

[52] Dillon, *Indian Wars*, 57.

Iroquois from the St. Lawrence. The Three Fires Confederacy was there as well as the Wyandotte from Sandusky and Detroit. Little Thunder almost certainly attended as the leading war chief of the Ahnishenahbek along with his two warrior sons. This was the largest Confederacy ever brought together by First Nations alone.

Meanwhile, the Big Knives kept trying to buy peace by sending delegations with offers of compensation but they were ignored. At the same time President Washington had called upon Major General Anthony Wayne (Mad Anthony) to raise a new army to finally complete what Harmar and St. Clair had failed to accomplish. It would be a much better disciplined much larger army numbering 5,120 officers, NCOs and privates. He began enlisting and drilling the new soldiers at Pittsburgh in June of 1792. Wayne was determined not to make the same mistake as his predecessors. He would take the time necessary to forge this new army into the crack troops required to defeat his enemies.

His army grew slowly as it moved deeper into First Nations' territory. He left Pittsburgh at the end of 1792 encamping at Legionville, some 22 miles south of Pittsburgh, where he stayed until the spring of 1793. From there he moved to Hobson's Choice, on the Ohio River between Cincinnati and Mill Creek, until finally making his headquarters near Fort Hamilton in October 1793. He was receiving new recruits daily and was drilling them and training them in the art of forest warfare.

First Nations' stunning successes on the Wabash and the Maumee Valley instilled terror in the hearts of their enemies. The army of the Big Knives suffered chronic desertion rates because their army was being assembled so close to First Nations country. Recruits were so apprehensive of danger that many deserted regularly at the first sign of trouble. This became such a big problem for Wayne that a reward was posted for the apprehension and return of any deserter. Upon conviction at a court martial they would be severely punished, usually by one hundred lashes on the bare back, or sometimes they were executed by firing squad. An entry into the Orderly Book Mss. Pittsburgh dated August 9th 1792 reads, "Deserters having become very prevalent among our troops, at this place, particularly upon the least appearance, or rather apprehension of danger, that some men (for they are unworthy of the name of soldiers), have lost in every sense of honor and duty as to desert their posts as sentries, by which treacherous, base and cowardly conduct, the lives and safety of their brave companions and worthy citizens were committed to savage fury."[53]

While Wayne took the time necessary to assemble his army and to drill them into the well disciplined military required to be successful against us attempts by the Big Knives at peace negotiations continued. President Washington appointed three commissioners to discuss terms of a peace treaty with us. They met at Niagara and availed themselves of the hospitalities of Lieutenant Governor Simcoe of Upper Canada until passage could be arranged to Sandusky. They hoped to meet in council there with our chiefs.

While the commissioners were travelling Washington requested the Mohawk chief Joseph Brant to go to the Miami where Little Turtles' Confederacy was in council. He arrived and tried to persuade them to send a delegation to Sandusky, meet the Big Knives' commissioners and to make a lasting peace with the United States. He was partly successful. They sent a delegation of about fifty to talk with the commissioners in front of Governor Simcoe. They parlayed with the commissioners for

---

[53] Burton C.M. *Anthony Wayne and the Battle of Fallen Timbers*, MPHSC, Vol. 31, 475.

several days demanding that they inform them of General Wayne's movements and if they were empowered to fix a permanent boundary line. Their answers must have proved satisfactory as the delegation agreed to meet them in council at Sandusky.

The commissioners, with a British escort, sailed for Sandusky following the north shore of Lake Erie to the mouth of the Detroit River where they made camp. Simcoe would not allow them to enter Detroit. Meanwhile another First Nations' delegation arrived from the Miami. They felt that their first delegation had not impressed clearly enough their position in regards to the boundary line. The second delegation made it crystal clear that they were insisting the original boundary line of the Ohio River, as negotiated in the Treaty of Stanwix, be adhered to and that all squatters remove themselves to the other side of the Ohio. The commissioners replied that they were only authorized to offer compensation for lands that now covered eastern and southern Ohio. White settlers had for some years been illegally establishing themselves with farms and villages in this part of First Nations' territory and they felt that it would be absolutely impossible for the United States government to now force them to move. This answer was not satisfactory to the council at the Miami.

After waiting some time the council sent a third delegation to the mouth of the Detroit with their final position on the article of the boundary line and a counter proposal on the removal of the squatters. The commissioners were informed that they would not be met at Sandusky, or anywhere else unless the Ohio River was first conceded as the boundary line between lands previously ceded and First Nations Territory.

As for the deportation of the illegal immigrants they proposed the following solution:

We know that these settlers are poor, or they would never have ventured to live in a country which has been in continual trouble ever since they crossed the Ohio. Divide, therefore, this large sum which you have offered us, among these people; give to each, also, a proportion of what you say you would give to us annually, over and above this very large sum of money, and we are persuaded they would most readily accept of it, in lieu of the lands you sold them. If you add, also, the great sums you must expend in raising and paying armies with a view to force us to yield you our country, you will certainly have more than sufficient for the purposes of repaying these settlers for all their labours and their improvements. You have talked to us about concessions. It appears strange that you should expect any from us, who have only been defending our just rights against your invasions. We want peace. Restore to us our country, and we shall be enemies no longer.[54]

This solution, although skilfully argued, would not even be considered. The Big Knives wanted the whole country and they would have it by any means even war. "The whole white race is a monster who is always hungry, and what he eats is land!" remarked Chicksika of the Shawanee.

While these attempts at arriving at a peaceful solution were going on Wayne had been busily moving west establishing several forts from Fort Washington to Fort Recovery. These would serve as support for his supply lines for the anticipated battles to come. On October 14th 1793 he reached the southwest branch of the Great Miami River where he camped

---

[54] Ibid.,480.

for the winter. The alliance made two successful raids on his supply lines that same month and then wintered at the Glaize.

That same year Britain and France had gone to war in Europe. In the spring of 1794 the new Governor of Canada Sir Guy Carlton was sure that the United States would soon side with France and Britain would be at war again with them. In preparation for such an event he had Fort Miami established on the Maumee River just north of the Glaize. He also strengthened fortifications on a small island at its mouth. This was very encouraging to the confederacy further stimulating its confidence. They thought if they did have to abandon their stronghold at the Glaize they could retreat to the safety of the new Fort Miami, run by the British.

Lieutenant Governor Simcoe visited us on the Maumee in April 1794 and told us that Britain would soon be at war with the Americans and that they would once again reassert their rights to lands south of the Great Lakes. They would scrap the Treaty of Fort Harmar, in which a few minor chiefs for a paltry $ 9,000 had ceded the territory the Big Knives were hungering for with no mention of a boundary line. All this was encouraging indeed. At last our great ally was about to spring into action and fully support our confederacy.

Wayne was encamped at Fort Greenville and had mustered an army of thirty-five hundred including fifteen hundred Kentucky Militiamen. Wayne's forces were greater in number and far more disciplined than any our confederacy had faced before. Wayne left Fort Greenville for the Glaize. Little Turtle grasped the situation more clearly than anyone else and gave his advice. "Do not engage the 'General that never sleeps' and instead sue for peace." His counsel was rejected so he capitulated the general leadership of our Confederation to Shawanee war chief Blue Jacket.

Blue Jacket left the Glaize with the intent of cutting Wayne's supply line behind Fort Greenville and he kept picking up warriors along the way. As he neared Fort Recovery he had a force of twelve hundred warriors with half of them being Three Fires members. This group wanted to attack Fort Recovery, which was weakly defended for psychological advantage, another defeat for General Wayne to think about. The plan did not go well as Blue Jacket did not support the Otahwah and Ahnishenahbek. The day was spent wasting ammunition taking pot shots at the defenders behind the stockade. At the end of the day their resolve disintegrated and they returned to the Glaize in deep division. The campaign to cut Wayne's supply lines never came to fruition.

An American deserter named Newman seeking refuge reached the Glaize the first week in August. He informed the alliance of the approach of Wayne's army so Blue Jacket ordered the Shawanee towns at the Glaize to evacuate down the Maumee to seek refuge along Swan Creek near present day Toledo. There was no time to mount a united defence so they fell back to a place on the Maumee that was strewn with trees downed by a recent tornado. This gave the place the name Fallen Timbers and it was here that the alliance prepared its defence. Wayne moved from the Glaize more quickly than the alliance anticipated and the warriors were caught off guard. Although fifteen hundred warriors were assembled they were not all at the ready. Some of the young warriors were off hunting as this was how they augmented British food supplies. Some were four miles away at Fort Miami picking up supplies of food and ammunition. In all there were perhaps only five hundred warriors at Fallen Timbers when Wayne arrived.

They fought bravely but were outnumbered six to one. Whenever they were about to be overrun they would retreat then re-establish a line of defence. This strategy continued until the warriors reached the closed gates of Fort Miami. Then the unthinkable happened!

Major William Campbell commanded Fort Miami and he had only a small garrison of redcoats. He had a tremendous decision to make. He was duty bound to defend the fort if attacked but if he opened the gates to give succour to Britain's allies he risked not only his own life but also those he was directly responsible for. Worst yet he risked plunging his country into war with the United States of America, a war they could not afford because they were already fully extended in Europe. He made his decision quickly refusing to open the gates of the fort to the mortification of the fleeing warriors. While peering over the stockade he is said to have called down to the pleading warriors, "I cannot let you in! You are painted too much my children!"[55] The warriors had no choice but to flee down the Maumee in full retreat.

The Battle of Fallen Timbers[56] broke the Confederacy. It established the United States as a bona fide nation because it decisively defeated Britain's most important ally along the frontier. One chronicler wrote that it was the most important battle ever won by the U.S. because it was Fallen Timbers that would make or break the fledgling nation. It showed how perfidious an ally Britain could be and Blue Jacket would complain years later, "It was then that we saw the British dealt treacherously with us".[57]

The Three Fires warriors returned to their villages in

---

[55] John Sugden, *Tecumseh* (New York: Henry Holt and Company, 1997), 90.
[56] For a complete report of this battle see Burton, *Anthony Wayne*, MPHSC, Vol. 31, 472-489.
[57] Sugden, *Tecumseh*, 90.

Michigan and Ontario. Never again would the Ahnishenahbek fight as a body independent and on their own. Now in his seventies Little Thunder had participated in his last campaign. It was not unusual for older men to have fought in the Indian Wars. For example, David Morgan was seventy when he defended his home against First Nation marauders. He was the brother of General Daniel Morgan who campaigned in the American Revolution.

Blue Jacket called the Confederacy's war chiefs to Fort Greenville the following year to treat for peace. Little Thunder answered his call and performed his final duty as a war chief by signing the Treaty of Greenville in 1795 (see Appendix 2).

8

Our Country is Being Eaten: 1795-1812

The Treaty of Greenville was first and foremost "A treaty of peace between the United States of America and the Tribes of Indians, called the Wyandots, Delawares, Shawanoes, Ottawas, Chipewas, Putawatimes, Miamis, Eel-River, Weea's, Kickapoos, Piankashaws and Kaskaskias. To put an end to a destructive war ..."[58] Throughout the wording of this treaty we are never referred to as nations but tribes only. Such was the mindset of the Big Knives.

Although it was primarily a peace treaty articles dealing with land cessions are included. Article 3 deals with a new boundary line that ceded all of eastern and southern present day Ohio to the U.S. This boundary line separating "the lands of the United States, and the lands of the said Indian tribes" had vastly

---

[58] Treaty of Greenville, August 3, 1795.

different meanings to the signatories. First Nations people wanted their own country but the Big Knives were setting the stage for future land grabs. Included in the United States' relinquishment of all "Indian lands northward of the River Ohio, eastward of the Mississippi, and westward and southward of the Great Lakes" is the cession of sixteen other tracts of lands each several miles square and rights of passage to them. These were scattered throughout the Northwest Territory where Forts were already established or where the Big Knives wished to establish towns. Article 5 defines relinquishment as it is applied to the United States. "The Indian tribes who have a right to those lands, are quietly to enjoy them ... but when those tribes ... shall be disposed to sell their lands ... they are to be sold only to the United States". In other words we did not have our "own country" but only the right to use certain lands already belonging to the Big Knives.

The Ahnishenahbek and Otahwah ceded from their territory on the Detroit River a strip of land from the River Raisin to Lake St. Clair six miles deep which included Detroit as well as a tract on the north shore of the Straits of Mackinaw including the Islands of Mackinaw and De Bois Blanc. And so with the Treaty of Greenville the erosion of Ahnishenahbek lands had begun.

During this time the Deputy Superintendent General for the Indian Department of the British Colonial Government was Alexander McKee. He had been an Indian Agent in the department for years and had traded with the Shawanee even before the American Revolution. Like all traders he lived among the First Nations and had married a Shawanee woman. McKee fought with us in the Revolutionary War organizing a war party, mostly of "Lake Indians", at the Shawanee Town of Pekowi for a successful raid into Kentucky. At McKee's town he had built a house with a brick chimney and had an orchard. He had a depot at the foot of the Miami Rapids in 1792 where British supplies for the Confederacy's war effort were received from Detroit.

In 1786 he had brokered a surrender treaty ceding a tract of land seven miles square on the south side of the Detroit River including Bois Blanc Island. The preamble reads in part "...for and in consideration of the goodwill, friendship and affection, which we have for Alexander McKee, who served with us against the enemy during the late war..."[59] Alexander McKee was a man highly respected among the First Nations and he generated a great deal of affection among us.

In 1795 McKee was stationed at Detroit. Just six weeks after the Treaty of Greenville was signed he met in council on the Thames River with six Ahnishenahbek chiefs. Lord Dorchester, Governor of Canada, had instructed him to purchase lands from us for the estimated three thousand First Nations refugees expected to arrive in Canada because of the late war. The chiefs enthusiastically accepted his plan to sell twelve square miles on the St. Clair River for this purpose and entered into a provisional agreement with him (See Appendix 2). This tract would eventually become Sombra Township.

He concurrently entered into a provisional agreement for a township at the forks of the Thames River (London). McKee said Lieutenant-Governor Simcoe wanted to establish Upper Canada's capital there because it would be easier to defend than York (Toronto). These provisional agreements were signed in September of that year on the Thames and the following year thirteen Ahnishenahbek chiefs, including Little Thunder, signed confirmatory Treaties Six and Seven. The purposes of these

---

[59] *Indian Treaties and Surrenders*, Treaty No. 116, vol. 1 (Toronto: Coles Publishing Company, 1992), 272

treaties were never carried out even though there was a large Otahwah village on the boundary of Sombra and both Muncie and Moravian Delaware had moved into Upper Canada looking for refuge.   In the 1830s there was a migration of Ahnishenahbek from Saginaw as well as a large influx of Potawatomi both looking for refuge but the Shawanese reserve had been opened up to white settlement.   Treaty Seven for Sombra Township is currently in the land claims process.

In the meantime the American "Northwest Territories" were filling up with white settlers.   This degraded traditional hunting grounds and impoverished First Nations.   Our brothers had spiralled into a cycle of poverty, selling off their land for a pittance, which only lead to more poverty.   The new republic clamoured for more land.   The settlers demanded more cessions because they did not trust their First Nations neighbours.   Land speculators were greedy for profit.   Political motivation spurred on the legislators.   By increasing the population of an individual territory it would not only provide more security for the whites it would increase the possibility of statehood.

The new Governor of Indiana Territory, William Henry Harrison, reacted to this clamour for more land with deft and unreasonable enthusiasm.   "Between 1802 and 1805 he concluded no less than seven treaties by which Delawares, Miamis, Weas, Piankeshaws, Eel Rivers, Potawatomis, Kickapoos, Shawnees, Kaskaskias, Sacs, and Foxes alienated their title to the southern part of Indiana, portions of Wisconsin and Missouri, and most of Illinois, all for the derisory sum of two cents and acre or less."[60]   Harrison hardly kept fairness in view while "negotiating" these treaties.   Such tactics as bribery, the threat of cancellation of annuities already agreed to and

---

[60] Sugden, *Tecumseh*, 106.

supplying liberal quantities of liquor were employed. Deals were struck with many First Nation individuals without regard to their authority to speak for their people.

Many American pioneers were moving into our country and squatting along the western shores of Lake St. Clair and the St. Clair River. Many farms dotted the shoreline north of Detroit. However, a few had resided here for many years as traders and trappers. These were not looked upon as squatters but were given deeds to land as gifts by the Ahnishenahbek. Little Thunder signed three such deeds, one to a William Tucker of Detroit on September 22, 1780 and a second to Richard Cornwall of Detroit on October 28, 1780. A third was signed on August 28, 1798 for a gift of land to William Thorn Jr.

Early in 1807 the United States turned its attention fully to Ahnishenahbek country. William Hull, the Governor of Michigan Territory received orders to negociate a treaty resulting in the ceding of Ahnishenahbek lands and the creation of reservations. Hull invited us along with the Wyandotte, Potawatomi and Otahwah of Detroit to meet with him in June. The First Nations flatly refused.

Trout, an apostle of Tecumseh's brother The Prophet, had been among the Ahnishenahbek at Michilimackinac claiming to speak the words of The Prophet. In his speech he declared that The Prophet pronounced "the Americans, but not other whites, to be the progeny of an evil spirit".[61] These words echoed the messages of both the widely admired and respected Tecumseh and The Prophet. First Nations were also angry that annuities due from the Treaty of 1805 had yet to be paid. Hull blamed mistakes by New York banks and he even tried to lay the blame at our feet claiming that we should have come to Detroit and

---

[61] Ibid., 158.

gotten our annuities at an earlier date. Also we were dismayed at realizing that the price being offered, less then a cent an acre, was far below the market value.

Hull went to Saginaw in June to meet with the Saginaw band. He was chastised by the head chief for wanting them to sell land to him after advising them not to sell land to anyone. He was then ordered never to return to Saginaw territory. Finally the annuities due arrived in July and Hull fully expected all the chiefs to come to Detroit in the fall, but the chiefs from Saginaw refused saying they had been advised to stand against any more land cessions by our Congress at Greenville.

In November 1807 the Treaty of Detroit was signed relinquishing upwards of five million acres of Michigan Territory including all of Aamjiwnaang territory west of the St. Clair (see appendix 1). Of the reservations set aside by this treaty two were located in St. Clair County. One tract three-mile square was located on the northwest shore of Lake St. Clair at Swan Creek. The other tract, two sections containing 1,287 acres, was on the Black River in what is now the west end of Port Huron. The residents of these two reservations would later be recognized as one band, the Chippewas of Swan Creek and Black River. One of the Ahnishenahbek signatories of the Treaty of Detroit was Little Thunder.

9

Needed Yet Again—The War of 1812

Once again the winds of war swept across "Indian Country". The British, realizing that they were vulnerable on the frontier were doing their best to win First Nations loyalty. "Indian presents" had doubled and they were anxious to know the standing of the First Nations. In February 1808 W. Claus of the Indian Department spoke with Chief Guyash of Bear Creek (Sydenham River) at Amherstburg. After a good deal of conversation he came to the point of the conference. He asked the chief directly what he thought the position of the First Nations would be if there should be any disturbance between the British and the Americans. Guyash told him the Three Fires generally felt they should remain neutral, not the answer he was looking for. The next day he met with an Otahwah chief called the little King from L'Arbre Croche. When asked the same question the wily Otahwah leader told him he would know if it happened. When pressed he said that most of the First Nations were decidedly against the Americans.

The Americans were doing their best to keep the First Nations out of the looming conflict. In August of 1809 Governor Hull addressed the Otahwah and Ahnishenahbek nations at Michilimackinac. The purpose was to pledge friendship by liberally distributing many valuable presents, medals bearing the president's image for the chiefs and American flags for them to fly in their villages. Included in his speech was a warning not to become allies with the British or the Shawnee Prophet, Tenskwatawa.

Some of the Governor's words that day probably damaged his cause more than the abundance of presents helped it. Hull encouraged the First Nations to abandon their way of life by presenting the example of their "brethren to the South [who] have changed their habits of life and instead of making hunting, fishing and idleness their principal pursuits…now attend to the cultivation of the land".[62]   They neither wanted to become farmers nor did they think that hunting and fishing provided them with more than ample idle time.

He also ordered them not to listen to the counsel of the British. Hull stated emphatically that it was their duty and in their interest to listen to the advice of the American Government saying, "your duty because you live in our Country; your interest because we are the only nation that can afford you protection".[63]   There he stood in unceded First Nation lands calling them his country and offering them protection that they never asked for nor did they need.

During this time the great Shawanee chief Tecumseh had moved his village from the lands ceded at Greenville to a location at the junction of the Wabash and the Tippecanoe

---

[62] *Gov. Hull's Address to the Indians*, Aug. 28, 1809, MPHSC, Vol. 8, 568.
[63] Ibid., 570.

Rivers. This new village, called Prophetstown after his brother, was to be the nerve centre for his operations. As a young warrior he had fought with Little Turtle and Blue Jacket's Confederacy against Harmar and St. Clair. He lost a brother at Fallen Timbers and he refused to sign the Treaty of Greenville because it ceded land. It was during this time that he caught the vision of a pan-First Nations Confederacy to stop American aggression. He never lost sight of that vision and he now saw the opportunity to advance his cause by taking advantage of the British's vulnerability on the frontier.

Help in uniting the First Nations came in the strangest way. William Henry Harrison had decided to put an end of the "Indian unrest and uprisings" in the new Northwest Territories. He decided to attack and destroy what he thought was the centre of all the unrest, Prophetstown. Tecumseh was away to the south spreading his vision and recruiting new members when Harrison arrived at Tippecanoe. Tenskwatawa, who he left in charge and with orders not to engage the Big Knives, saw an opportunity and attacked first. He convinced his warriors that his medicine had made the enemy's "powder turn to sand" and his "bullets turn to mud" so they would be invincible.

Harrison countered with enough success to make Prophetstown's warriors abandon the village. Although casualties were about equal Harrison claimed the victory, burned the town and carried off what booty he could. The Prophet lost a great deal prestige that day. Tecumseh was furious and the British gained a staunch ally. Instead of ending the turmoil Harrison only drove the First Nations into unfaltering loyalty to the British cause.

The Michigan pioneers were terror stricken because of a lack of protection against impending First Nations attacks, so much so that they sent a Memorial[64] to congress outlining their fears and demanding extra troops to protect them. They didn't fear the British army but wondered if they could trust them for compassion should they have to turn to them. "Is there again a refuge for the helpless in flight? On the south the savages intercept them…on the west, on the north, they perfectly surround them. Shall they then lift an eye to the east, throw themselves on the mercy of the British, and will they, or can they, there, find mercy?"[65]

In 1811 Henry Clay's war hawks gained control of the Congress. The land hungry Americans coveted the balance of Britain's North American territories and saw a weakness they could exploit. Great Britain had expended much of her resources on the Napoleonic Wars in Europe and her means of defending her North America possessions were minimal. They war hawks laid the blame for the frontier violence squarely at the feet of the British. They used the pretence that the British continually instigated First Nation alliances against them. This, along with the accusations of the continual impressments of American sailors at sea, led to the War of 1812.

At first the Ahnishenahbek showed little interest in the many calls for support issued from Amherstburg or in Tecumseh's vision or in being active allies of the British in a war with the Big Knives. They could see how weak the British were along the frontier and how the Big Knives outnumbered both parties. The province of Upper Canada had a population of seventy-seven thousand while the American Northwest was enumerated at six hundred and seventy-seven thousand. However, as tensions heightened a few Detroit Ahnishenahbek

---

[64] *Memorial to Congress by Citizens of Michigan Territory*, December 10, 1811, MPHSC, Vol. 9, 346-353.
[65] Ibid., 350.

joined the three hundred and fifty First Nation warriors gathered on Bois Blanc Island in front of Amherstburg. They were mostly Wyandotte from the east side of the Detroit led by Roundhead, Split Log and Warrow and Potawatomi under Main Poc with a few Menominee, Winnebago, Sioux, Munsees and Otahwah. Tecumseh was also there with a few warriors from the Wabash.

At first things looked grim for Upper Canada. Only three hundred men of the 41st Regiment of Foot, six hundred Canadian militiamen and our small force of three hundred and fifty warriors protected the border. On July 12, 1812 Brigadier-General William Hull invaded our country at Sandwich (Windsor) unopposed. The few regulars and four hundred and fifty volunteers that were there to protect Sandwich scrambled back to Fort Malden (Amherstburg). The next day Hull issued a proclamation to the "Inhabitants of Canada" in which he presented the American army as liberators from tyranny and assured Canadian citizens he would respect their property if they remained neutral. However, his anxiety over First Nation warriors showed through with his zero tolerance warning that "No white man found fighting at the side of an Indian will be taken prisoner: Instant destruction will be his lot."[66]

Hull could have swept Malden away and marched uncontested to Niagara and General Brock's flank, but he didn't. He was a veteran of the Revolutionary War and as a younger soldier much more daring. He had become overly cautious and vacillating in his old age. He worried about his supply line, the road from Maumee to Detroit, and he had visions of "hordes of savages" descending upon him.

Colonel Lewis Cass took the Aux Canard Bridge, which led

---

[66] Sugden, *Tecumseh*, 284.

to Amherstburg. Our warriors harassed Cass's Ohio Militia with wasp-like sorties and Hull fretted over his supply line being broken, so he did the unexplainable. He ordered Cass to return to Sandwich so they burned the only bridge leading to Fort Malden and Hull withdrew his forces from Canada retreating to the safety of Fort Detroit.

We began to enjoy successes against the Big Knives. We switched our operations to the west side of the Detroit and hemmed up Hull's supplies at Frenchtown (Monroe, MI). We surrounded the pro-American Wyandotte villages of Maguaga and Brownstown, which protected Hull's supply line from Ohio and spirited the inhabitants away to the east side of the Detroit. A council was held and Tecumseh, using his extraordinary charisma and oratory skills convinced Walk-in-the-Water and his people to abandon the Americans and join the confederacy. This added about eighty warriors to our forces and further demoralized General Hull. It also enabled us to cut his supply line leaving him stranded in Detroit.

News of the happenings around Detroit spread throughout our territories. Our feelings of concern over a war with the Big Knives began to melt away. Our small force on the Detroit had shown they could be beaten. That very month a group of warriors from Aamjiwnaang left for Amherstburg. War chiefs Red Sky of Black River, Quakegman of the St. Clair band and Waupugais from the Sauble would have probably led them. They travelled down the St. Clair picking up more warriors from Lake St. Clair led by such war chiefs as Petahwegeeshig and Quaquakeboogk. When they arrived at Amherstburg they attached themselves to Tecumseh and his confederacy. More Ahnishenahbek arrived. War chiefs such as Miscocomon from the Thames, Kaynotang from Bear Creek and great warriors like Okemos and Manitocorbway from Cedar River (Lansing,

Michigan) swelled our forces to six hundred warriors.

Things happened quickly in July 1812. Colonel Henry Proctor had succeeded Lieutenant-Colonel Thomas Bligh St. George as commandant of Fort Malden. Then an anticipated attack by American forces at Niagara was delayed and Major-General Isaac Brock arrived at Fort Malden with reinforcements. Fort Michilimackinac had fallen without a shot being fired. Apparently Otahwah and Ahnishenahbek warriors were on their best behaviour following its capitulation. Mr. Askin Jr. in an unaddressed letter wrote, "I never saw so determined a set of people as the Chippewas & Ottawas were. Since the capitulation they have not drunk a single drop of Liquor, nor even Killed a Fowl belonging to any person (a thing never Known before) for they generally destroy everything they meet with."[67]

All of this only served to heighten Hull's trepidation bringing him nearer to the breaking point. With the fall of Michilimackinac he expected "a large body of Savages from the north...that the British can engage any number of Indians...and that, including the engagements of the N.W. and S.W. Companies two or three thousand will be brought to this place in a very short time".[68] His supply line had been cut off. His son, daughter and grandchildren were with him and he feared for their lives. He had sent relief to the River Raisin so his supplies could get through but our warriors forced them back. He was facing mutiny among his troops and he was cracking.

Brock was a daring commander and somewhat cavalier in thought. He decided to take advantage of Hull's vulnerability by undertaking a colossal bluff. He sent a demand to Hull to surrender Detroit, which included the warning that he could not

---

[67] Askin, John. *Michilimackinac 18ᵗʰ July 1812.* MPHSC, Vol. 15, 113.
[68] *William Hull to William Eustis,* MPHSC, Vol. 40, 434.

guarantee that he would be able to control First Nation warriors if he refused. Hull did refuse so we crossed the Detroit south of the American fort and attacked it head on. Warriors paraded in full view of the fort by filing out of a wooded area, all the time screeching blood-curdling war hoops, and then disappearing into the woods on the other side only to return to the beginning point via the rear. Around and around we went making our six hundred look like the thousands Hull feared. The psychological damage caused Hull to capitulate by sending out his son with a white flag. Detroit fell August 16, 1812 with only a few canon shots fired by both sides.

After the fall of Detroit even more Ahnishenahbek warriors joined the confederacy. Eshtonaquet arrived with a group from Swan Creek, as did Naiwash from Sahgeeng. Our numbers began to soar. It was us and not the British that kept on the offensive that fall with stinging attacks at Pigeon Roost in Indiana, Fort Madison near St. Louis and Fort Harrison north of Vincennes.

Hull's surrender was on a par with "St. Clair's shame". He was charged with treason, cowardice, and neglect of duty and bad conduct. At his court martial in the spring of 1814 he was cleared of the charges of treason and cowardice but found guilty of neglect of duty and bad conduct. Hull was sentence to be shot, however mercy was recommended because of his age and previous excellent military record. President Madison remitted his sentence. William Hull spent the rest of his life virtually an outcast trying to make his case and defend himself. He died in 1825.

When news of the American disaster at Detroit reached Washington, D.C., William Henry Harrison was chosen as commander of the western army and he was issued new orders. When he had gathered a new force of ten thousand he was to retake Detroit then penetrate as far into Canada as possible. He began to collect supplies and recruits at St. Marys (Girty's Town) sending them on in stages to the collection point at the rapids of the Maumee River. He wanted to use the thick winter ice on the Detroit to cross over and attack Fort Malden directly.

At the end of December he sent forward Brigadier-General James Winchester with thirteen hundred men. When he arrived he received urgent word from the inhabitants of Frenchtown on the River Raisin pleading for protection from First Nation warriors. He heeded the calls for help by sending forward Colonel Will Lewis with five hundred and fifty men quickly followed by Colonel John Allen with one hundred and ten more. Two days later Winchester arrived with three hundred more. That same day six hundred warriors and five hundred soldiers led by Proctor crossed the ice from Amherstburg to Brownstown and headed down the road toward Frenchtown.

The Americans, civilians and military alike dreaded our Confederacy. The following depiction of our warriors was given by Major Richardson, of the 41st Regiment on their way to Frenchtown that January 1813:

> No other sound than the measured step of the troops interrupted the solitude of the scene, rendered more imposing by the appearance of the warriors, whose bodies, stained and painted in the most frightful manner for the occasion, glided by us with almost noiseless velocity; some painted white, some black, others half black and half red, half black and half white; all with their hair plastered in such a way as to resemble the bristling quills of the porcupine, with no other covering than a cloth around their loins, yet armed to the teeth with rifles, tomahawks, war clubs, spears, bows and arrows, and scalping knives.

Uttering no sound, and intent on reaching the enemy
unperceived ...[69]

Colonel Proctor said, in his dispatch to Sir G. Provost,
"After suffering, for our numbers, a considerable loss, the
enemy's force posted in the houses and enclosures, which from
dread of falling into the hands of the Indians, they most
obstinately defended, at length surrendered at discretion; the
other part of their force in attempting to retreat by the way they
came, were, I believe, all, or with very few exceptions, killed by
the Indians."[70]

The Big Knives were not situated well and our warriors
mauled them badly. Roundhead captured Winchester and after
being forced to watch some of our warriors perform their craft
he was persuaded to sign an order directing four hundred of his
men to surrender. The Major in charge refused unless Proctor
would guarantee their safety, which he did. Winchester was
then turned over to Proctor. That day the Big Knives lost three
hundred killed, twenty-seven wounded and their entire army
save a handful taken prisoner. Proctor, fearing Harrison and his
advancing reinforcements scampered back across the ice to
Malden. As he left he was asked about medical help for the
wounded Americans and he is said to have replied, "The Indians
are excellent doctors".[71] The River Raisin battle was another
disaster for the Big Knives.

---

[69] Lady Matilda Ridout Edgar, Lady. *Ten Years of Upper Canada in Peace and
War, 1805-1815; being The Ridout Letters* (Toronto: William Briggs, 1890),
174 available at
http://www.canadiana.org/ECO/ItemRecord/02885?id=4fa228b7f317e
943 last accessed 22 June 2006.
[70] Ibid.
[71] John K. Mahon, *The War of 1812* (New York: Da Cappo Press Inc.
1991), 130.

Proctor left a minimal guard to protect the wounded Americans but they weren't up to the task. It was reported that after some celebratory festivities, which included too much liquor consumption about fifty of our warriors attacked, killed and mutilated thirty-three of the eighty sick and wounded captives.

The Big Knives charged that prisoners were inhumanely massacred. Proctor, who was promoted to Brigadier-General, complained about warrior conduct to his superiors blaming liquor and his subordinate for not preventing it. The superintendent informed the allieance about the complaint in July at a Grand-Council held at Ten Mile Creek. Chief Blackbird of Manitoulin answered for us eloquently presenting our views on the conduct of war and the treatment of prisoners.

> At the foot of the Rapids (Grand Rapids, Michigan) last spring we fought the Big Knives and we lost some of our people there. When we retired the Big Knives got some of our dead. They were not satisfied with having killed them, but cut them into small pieces. This made us very angry. My words to my people were: 'As long as the powder burnt [the fighting continued], to kill and scalp,' but those behind us came up and did mischief [by shooting the Indians after the surrender]. Brother, last year at Chicago and St. Joseph's the Big Knives destroyed all our corn. This was fair, but, brother, they did not allow the dead to rest. They dug up their graves, and the bones of our ancestors were thrown away and we never could find them to return them to the ground. Brother, I have listened with a good deal of attention to the wish of our father. If the Big Knives, after they kill people of our colour, leave them without hacking them to

pieces, we will follow their example. They have themselves to blame. The way they treat our killed, and the remains of those that are in their graves in the west, makes our people mad when they meet the Big Knives. Whenever they get any of our people into their hands they cut them like meat into small pieces. We thought white people were Christians. They ought to show us a better example. We do not disturb their dead. What I say is known to all the people present. I do not tell a lie. Brother, it is the Indian custom when engaged [in war] to be very angry, but when we take prisoner to treat them kindly...Brother, the officer that we killed, you have spoken to us before about. I now tell you again, he fired and wounded one of our colour, and another fired at him and killed him. We wished to take him prisoner, but the officer said 'God damn' and fired, when he was shot. That is all I have to say.[72]

Were the sick and wounded prisoners at Frenchtown massacred by a small band of "drunken, carousing Indians"? Blackbird doesn't mention that version in his answer but says it was our way to treat prisoners kindly. Ridout seems to attribute the killing of wounded captives to escape attempts, "No doubt atrocities were committed by the Indians in spite of the efforts of their chiefs, who are said to have behaved well. A paper of 2nd February (Chilicothe Journal) says, 'Those who had surrendered on the field were taken prisoner, those who attempted escape were tomahawked.'"[73] Regardless of the truthfulness of any atrocities committed these stories were

[72] Schmalz, *Ojibwa*, 115.
[73] Edgar, *Ten Years*, 173.

believed by the Kentucky militia and gave rise to their battle cry "Remember the Raisin!"

On May 1, 1813 Proctor began a siege on Fort Meigs near the mouth of the Maumee. The alliance joined him with twelve hundred warriors. Harrison was in command of the fort, which was extremely well built and able to withstand a long siege. The allies were able to do little more the pelt the fortification with small arms fire while the British pounded it with heavy artillery, all to no avail. Our warriors became restless and our chiefs began to question Proctor's abilities.

This state of affairs continued for four days but then the situation changed. Reinforcements from Kentucky, which Harrison was waiting for, were spotted approaching up river. Brigadier-General Green Clay was at the rapids with fourteen hundred men. Harrison sent orders to split the force in two. Six hundred under General Clay were to fight their way into the fort while the other eight hundred under Colonel William Dudley were to outflank the British batteries and spike their cannons then retreat to the fort. Both were successful in their objectives but Dudley got carried away.

First Nation warriors had been engaging Green Clay on the other side of the fort but when they realized what Dudley was up to they quickly swam the river and began to attack him from the forest. Dudley foolishly followed them deeper into the woods. This kind of combat led to the killing of Dudley while his regiment fled to the British line in order to surrender. Many Americans were cut down while in flight and many more were taken prisoner.

The prisoners were sent by the British under a guard of fifty men to be held at the old ruins of Fort Miami. We, being in a highly agitated state and very angry, pestered the prisoners as they were being escorted to the holding area. After they arrived a few of our young men began to make some of the prisoners run the gauntlet. Some of them were killed, one a British regular trying to protect the prisoners. Things were getting out of hand. An urgent call for help went out and Tecumseh and Matthew Elliott rushed to the scene. An angry Tecumseh got our young warriors under control and they eventually dispersed. An Ahnishenahbek warrior named Split Nose is said to have instigated the whole affair. This incident gave him the reputation of being "a worthless Ojibwa" while Tecumseh's actions only served to bolster his already bigger-than-life status. [74]

The siege was given up at this point. The weather was bad the whole time, so General Proctor blamed the rain for the failure of the siege. He also blamed his superior General DeRottenburg for not providing extra men and supplies. We embarked on a journey home to celebrate our victory, which was our custom. Using the islands strung out across the south end of Lake Erie we made good time in reaching Aamjiwnaang.

That summer in a council we determined to clean the area of American supporters. A woman from Aamjiwnaang, because of some kindness shown to her, warned settlers that their lives were in danger. They left at once by boat for the safety of Detroit. On the way they met two men who were on their way back from a trip downriver, a Mr. King who was a settler on the east side of the St. Clair and a Mr. Rodd. These men did not perceive the height of the danger and determined that it was safe for them to continue home, Mr King being an Englishman and Mr. Rodd being half Ahnishenahbek and married to an Ahnishenahbi-kwe. They were mistaken.

While patrolling the waterways four of our warriors, Old

---

[74] Sugden, *Tecumseh*, 334-338.

Salt, Black Foot, Wabos or The Rabbit, a nanandawi healer, and Wawanosh came across them and mistook them for American sympathizers. In their rashness Wawanosh shot King and Rodd was also killed. Their families were brought to the village at the mouth of the St. Clair where the mistake was discovered and they were released.

By July we amassed again at Amherstburg with even more warriors joining us from the northwest. Robert Dickson, a tall Scot with flaming red hair, had been appointed Indian Agent because of his good relations with the First Nations. He had promised to recruit more warriors for the war effort and he proved true to his word. He paddled out of Lake St. Clair leading fourteen hundred warriors recruited from his base at Le Bay (Green Bay). They consisted of Ahnishenahbek, Sioux, Menominee, Potawatomi and Winnebago and raised our confederacy's number to twenty-five hundred.

This large group wanted to return to Fort Meigs but Proctor wanted to attack Fort Stephenson on the Sandusky. Tecumseh prevailed and they left for Fort Meigs July 19th.

The second siege of the formidable fort at the Maumee didn't go any better than the first. The Big Knives were continually popping up, shooting through their loopholes and disappearing again. To the warriors they looked like so many groundhogs. Harrison who had moved up the Sandusky left Green Clay in charge of Fort Meigs. A stratagem designed to lure Green Clay out of the fort failed, as did one to lure Harrison from his position on the Sandusky.

While the siege was underway Proctor decided to take Fort Stephenson anyway. He sent part of his forces with a few hundred of our warriors to the much weaker fort. While it was being assailed a scouting party of eighteen Ahnishenahbek including Okemos and his cousin Manitocorbway moved up the

Sandusky looking for any signs of Harrison's Big Knives. Okemos was a nephew of the great Otahwah chief Pontiac and like his uncle a redoubtable warrior. He described what happened in battle to Judge Littlejohn of Michigan Territory.

> One morning while lying in ambush near a road lately cut for the passage of the American army and supply wagons, we saw twenty cavalrymen approaching us. Our ambush was located on a slight ridge, with brush directly in our front. We immediately decided to attack the Americans, although they outnumbered us. Our plan was first to fire and cripple them, and then make a dash with the tomahawk. We waited until they came so near that we could count the buttons on their coats, when firing commenced. The cavalrymen, with drawn sabres, immediately charged upon the Indians. The plumes of the cavalrymen looked like a flock of a thousand pigeons just hovering for a lighting. Myself and my cousin fought side by side, loading and firing, while dodging from one cover to another. In less than ten minutes after the firing began the sound of a bugle was heard, and casting our eyes in the direction of the sound, we saw the roads and woods filled with cavalry. The Indians were immediately surrounded, and every man cut down. All were left for dead upon the field. Myself and my cousin had our skulls cloven, and our bodies gashed in a fearful manner. The cavalrymen, before leaving the field, in order to be sure life was extinct, would lean forward from their horses and pierce the breasts of the Indians, even into their lungs. The last I remember is, that after emptying one saddle, and springing toward another soldier, with clubbed rifle raised to strike, my head felt as if pierced with a

red-hot iron, and I went down from a heavy sabre-cut. All knowledge ceased from this time until many moons afterward, when I found myself nursed by the squaws of friends, who had found me where I fell, two or three days after the engagement. The squaws thought all were dead; but upon moving the bodies of myself and Manitocorbway, signs of life appeared, and we were taken to a place of safety, where we were nursed until restored to partial health.[75]

After his recovery Okemos was make a chief of the Shiawaaee Ahnishenahbek. He withdrew from the war and gave his allegiance to the United States of America. He would later negotiate with Michigan Territorial Governor Lewis Cass at Detroit after the Battle of Moraviantown.

Both sieges failed and Harrison was not engaged so Proctor withdrew. Many of Dickson's new recruits abandoned the field since there was not booty to be had. We also returned home travelling in two large canoes. It was after dark when we approached the St. Clair River. As we neared Harsen Island we were overcome by a sudden thunderstorm and one of our canoes overturned, dumping sixteen warriors into the water. Most made it to the shore across from the Harsen homestead. A Mrs. Graveraet was visiting her brother at the Harsen farmhouse and the loud whoops calling to our lost companions frightened her terribly. She wanted to take her brother's baby and leave but he convinced her to stay.

The calls continued most of the night and all but two were able to find the shore in the darkness. The next morning we crossed over to the island our faces blackened with charcoal. We were in mourning for the two friends that we lost in the

---

[75] *History of St. Clair County*, A.T. Andreas, 189.

freak storm. We visited with the Harsen family for a while describing to them the battle at the Sandusky and how the sudden storm had burst upon us. The Harsens had been good friends and traders with us so we advised them to leave because we thought the Big Knives might be approaching. Then we continued our journey up river.[76]

The first year of the war had not gone well for the Big Knives. Even the British fiascos at Forts Meigs and Stephenson had little effect on our morale. But the direction of the war was about to change.

Up to this point the British had control of the lakes. However, the Big Knives were busily building a fleet of war ships at Presque Isle (Erie, Pennsylvania). The British were building more ships at Amherstburg to bring their Lake Erie fleet up to par. The American fleet was under command of Master Commandant Oliver Hazard Perry, the British under Captain Robert Heriot Barclay. Barclay was a captain with sea warfare experience and had lost an arm at Trafalgar; however, his six ships lacked experienced sailors. Each ship had only ten so General Proctor had to supply 250 redcoats to bring the fleet up to full strength. We supplied two warriors to act as marksmen when the expected battle moved to close quarters.

The British fleet sailed down the Detroit and out onto Lake Erie September 9, 1813. The next day at noon they met the Big Knives near the Bass Islands. Thunderous cannonade from a desperate battle on the lake could be heard, but not witnessed. It continued for three hours, then nothing.

At the same time the alliance was aware of the army Harrison was building and when he moved north they planned to stop him at the Huron River south of Detroit. They were

---

[76] Ibid., 182.

sure they could defeat him; after all they had done it before, as well as the armies of Hull, Winchester and Clay. But the British were acting strangely and they could sense something was wrong. Then they received a report that some soldiers had been seen throwing part of the wall of Fort Malden into the ditch! This could only mean one thing. The fort was being dismantled and the British were planning a retreat.

Proctor was inaccessible so they asked his second-in-command, Lieutenant-Colonel Warburton what was going on. He replied he didn't know and he seemed sincere. For several days they could get no answers. The chiefs were very agitated and the grumbling about British treachery grew louder with each passing day.   Finally Proctor agreed to meet with them in council. Tecumseh was their spokesman:

> Listen! When war was declared, our Father [Proctor] stood up and gave us the tomahawk, and told us he was now ready to strike the Americans; that he wanted our assistance; and that he certainly would get us our lands back which the Americans had taken from us. Listen! You told us at that time to bring forward our families to this place. We did so, and you promised to take care of them, and that they should want for nothing while the men would go and fight the enemy...When we last went to the rapids [Fort Meigs] it is true we gave you little assistance. It is hard to fight people who live like groundhogs. Father, listen! We know that our fleet has gone out. We know they have fought. We have heard the great guns, but know nothing of what has happened to Our Father with One Arm...We are astonished to see our Father tying up everything and preparing to run...without letting his red children know what his intentions are...and we

are sorry to see our Father doing so without seeing the
enemy...Listen Father! The Americans have not yet
defeated us by land; neither are we sure they have
done so by water. We, therefore, wish to remain here
and fight our enemy should they make their
appearance. Father! You have got the arms and
ammunition, which our Great Father [the King] sent
for his red children. If you have an idea of going
away, give them to us, and you may go...Our lives are
in the hands of the Great Spirit. We are determined to
defend our lands, and if it is his will, we wish to leave
our bones upon them.[77]

Such were the words of the great Shawnee chieftain. For
some reason Proctor was leaving not only his officers, but his
First Nations allies in the dark. Although embarrassed at the
council by Tecumseh's words he was able to extradite himself by
promising an answer in two days.

Tecumseh received word requesting his presence at a
meeting with Proctor and his officers. When he arrived the
British were gathered around a table with a map of the Detroit
area laid upon it. Proctor then informed Tecumseh of the news
that he had received a week earlier, that Barclay had been totally
vanquished, and exactly what that meant. With the Americans
in complete control of Lake Erie they had the ability to cut his
main supply line (Lake Erie) starving the British Right Division
of supplies. They even had the ability of preventing supplies
from reaching the Detroit on the secondary line (the Thames)
by sailing their warships above Fort Malden. Proctor's plan was
to retreat up the Thames and make a stand at the forks.

Tecumseh perceived the problem immediately. He agreed

---

[77] Sugden, *Tecumseh*, 359-360.

to parlay with our other chiefs and convince them to join the retreat, which they did. However, Proctor should have been forthright with us at once.

So the long retreat up the Thames River began and the American forces advanced across the border. Two days before the Battle of Moraviantown the Confederacy tested the Big Knives at McGregor's Creek in order to delay their advance. Red Sky would likely have participated along with our other chiefs and fifteen hundred warriors. The American general, Harrison, brought more than three thousand men up the Thames. The warriors tried to destroy the bridges that spanned the creek. They succeeded in burning the upper bridge, about a mile from the mouth of the creek but the larger bridge at the mouth was too wet to burn. They had to be satisfied by just pulling up its planks. This skirmish lasted about two hours and then the alliance's lines broke. Tecumseh was wounded in the arm and many of the warriors were scattered. The next day only five hundred warriors formed the battle lines.[78]

Proctor fled as soon as the encounter began. "Five minutes after the first shock Proctor's troops were flying in all directions. We are told that the General, without making an attempt to rally his men, fled in his carriage, hotly pursued by the enemy..."[79] The warriors stood their ground but they were under attack from Richard Mentor Johnson's regiment of one thousand mounted Kentucky volunteers. Edgar wrote of the warriors, "They waited until the enemy was within a few paces of them, and then hurled on them a deadly shower of bullets. In this part of the field the undergrowth was so thick that the mounted riflemen could not advance. They were therefore ordered to carry on the fight on foot...For a while victory hung in the

[78] Ibid., 366.
[79] Edgar, *Ten Years*, 232.

balance, but at last the great leader, Tecumseh, fell, and then his followers gave way and scattered through the woods."[80]

This event effectively broke the First Nations Confederacy and many left the conflict and returned home. Unfortunately what was left of the Confederacy was irregular and unorganized. Naiwash of Saugeen complained in October 1814, "We Indians ... from the westward, perhaps the Master of Life would give us more luck if we would stick together as we formerly did ... and we probably might go back and tread again upon our own lands. Chiefs and warriors, since our great chief Tecumtha has been killed we do not listen to one another. We do not rise together. We hurt ourselves by it. It is our own fault ... We do not, when we go to war, rise together, but we go one or two, and the rest say they will go tomorrow."[81]   Some of the warriors of Aamjiwnaang, such as Wawanosh, chose to fight on and participated with others in such battles as Lundy's lane.[82]

A Shawanee family resided on Little Bear Creek (North Sydenham River) near Wallaceburg and consisted of five brothers, all burly young warriors. One of them was Megish who fell at Lundy's Lane July 25, 1814. His mother always maintained that her son had gotten between the opposing armies, was fired upon by the Big Knives and was killed.

Chesby Blake, an American lake captain, had joined Winfield Scott's forces along with his crew. He relates the story of "the death of an Indian at Lundy's Lane, saying that as the two armies were approaching, and a little while before the action, an Indian was seen running swiftly between the opposing lines. The Captain of the company said: "'Blake, can't you kill

---

[80] Ibid., 233.

[81] Sugden, *Tecumseh*, 384.

[82] Greg Curnoe, *Deeds/Nations*, ed. Frank Davey and Neal Farris (London, ON: London Chapter, OAS, Occasional Publication #4, 1996), 157.

that Indian?' Blake fired, but without effect; reloading, he took steady aim, fired, and the fleeing savage was seen to leap upward, and then to fall dead." Undoubtedly the slain Shawnee was Megish and it was Captain Blake that killed him.[83]

The War of 1812 closed the door on one era and opened the door to another, one far less egalitarian. It was the last time the Ahnishenahbek were looked upon as allies. A new relationship began with the British, the era of land surrenders and with it the creation of the reserve system.

As a footnote to the war it may be said that not all Ahnishenahbek warriors fought on the side of the British. The redheaded Dickson who had supplied so many warriors from west of Lake Michigan insulted a Pillager Ahnishenahbek chief named Flat Mouth while recruiting in the west. The Lakota chief Shappa had killed two of Flat Mouth's cousins so his principal warrior Shawakeshig killed the Sioux chief and two others. Dickson was married to Shappa's sister so he sent a message to Flat Mouth saying he would no longer trade with his village and it would be swept away within four years. This alienated the Pillager band and they sided with the Big Knives.[84] Warren devotes a whole chapter to the Ahnishenahbek rejection of British overtures in the Minnesota district sub-titled, "Endeavours of the British to Entice the Ojibway of Lake Superior and Mississippi to Join Their Arms in the War of 1812" [85]

Another Chief loyal to the Big Knives was Wing of Mackinaw. When Michilimackinac fell he refused to help and influenced his whole band to remain neutral. It was Wing, who

---

[83] *History of St. Clair County*, A.T. Andreas, 181.
[84] William W. Warren, *History of the Ojibway People* (St. Paul: Borealis Books, Minnesota Historical Society Press, 1984), 362-363.
[85] Ibid., 368-377.

with eight strong warriors to paddle his canoe, travelled from Mackinaw to Detroit in order to advise Hull of the northern fort's capitulation.[86] Two Otahwah war chiefs who fought alongside the Big Knives were Late Wing and Shawbenee from L'Arbre Croche. Late Wing became a great friend of Governor Lewis Cass and Shawbenee travelled extensively throughout the United States after the war. "This privilege was granted to him by the Government of the United States for his patriotism and bravery." [87]

Closer to home one of our warriors on the Black River named John Riley personally sided with the Americans as did his two brothers, Peter and James. Their father was a German and their mother Ahnishenahbi-kwe, Menawcamegoqua, from Saginaw. The Rileys with a few others referred to as the Riley band were friendly to the Americans giving them much aid during the war. It is believed that John Riley acted as a guide to General Cass in repelling one of our attacks in the suburbs of Detroit in 1812 and that he shot one of our warriors during our advance. He also acted as an official interpreter for the Americans at Detroit in 1815.

As a reward for services rendered each brother received large tracts of land (640 acres) each in article three of the 1819 Treaty of Saginaw. Riley Township in St. Clair County was named after the family. The Americans referred to John Riley as a chief and they also referred to the Black River Reservation as the Riley Reservation. He lived in a house on the Black River on the northeast corner of the reserve (presently the corner of

[86] *History of St. Clair County*, A.T. Andreas, 183.
[87] Andrew J. Blackbird, *History of the Ottawa and Chippewa Indians of Michigan* (Ypsilanti, MI: The Ypsilanti Job Printing House, 1887), 26 available at http://www.canadiana.org/ECO/PageView?id=a31b3e758e50350b&display=00429+0003 last accessed 27 June 2006.

Water Street and Military Trail, Port Huron) until its surrender in 1836. That same year the Rileys sold their land at Saginaw and John Riley moved to Muncie Town on the Thames where he died in 1842.

Black Snake was another old chief of the Black River band. He had a daughter who married a strongly built young warrior named Black Duck who was a member of the Riley band. Black Duck had attached great affections to the Big Knives and seldom would any word against them go unchallenged.

In the spring of 1816 the Black River band held a Great Feast at the mouth of the Black River. Numerous warriors attended from the village on the east side of the St. Clair. They were invited guests as were Riley's American sympathizers. The celebrations went on for some time with many giving speeches. One young warrior from the village across the river gave a fine speech but ended it by bragging about his skill in battle and of all the Big Knives' scalps he took during the late war.

Black Duck said nothing until the boast was complete then rose to his feet, tomahawk in hand and said, "You are a great brave; you have killed many Americans; you have taken their scalps. They whom you killed were my friends, and you shall kill no more!"[88] He then tomahawked his guest killing him instantly. This abruptly ended the feast.

Black Duck knew that the relations of the slain visitor would soon be out for his blood to avenge their relative so he appealed to Governor Cass for security. He was placed in Fort Gratiot for his own protection and the governor turned to John Riley to mediate the situation. Riley negotiated a settlement with the family of the dead man by offering them an amount of money

---

[88] Jenks, *St. Clair County*, 176.

equal to the warrior's worth as well as extra goods from the public store at Detroit. They accepted but also demanded forty quarts of whiskey to help them grieve more easily and to help make the tears flow more freely. Governor Cass immediately ordered the money, goods and whiskey to be paid.

10

Now the British Want Our Lands: 1818-1827

After the war we settled back into our traditional lifestyle only using the two reservations in the spring and summer as fishing camps. Despite the ceding of our lands in Michigan Territory we still roamed throughout our territory wintering in our hunting camps and visiting our sugar bushes. But this wasn't to last for long. With more and more settlers arriving our hunting grounds in Michigan were being ruined and the continual ill feelings between us made it impossible to continue with our traditional way of life. Many crossed over to live on the east side of the St. Clair including Little Thunder. However, Red Sky stayed on the west side of the river.

A council was held at Amherstburg October 16, 1818[89] to inform the chiefs of "Chenaille Ecarte, River St. Clair, Sable &

---

[89] Robertson to Bowels, *Indian Council* MPHSC, Vol. 16, 643-644.

Thames & Bear Creek, vizt." that the Province of Upper Canada wanted "…to purchase all the Lands belonging to them the Chippewas lying north of the River Thames, including the River au Sable…" to which our chiefs replied that they were willing to sell their lands but asked "to make the following reserves: Four miles square at some distance below the rapids of the River St. Clair, one mile in front by four deep bordering on said river & adjoining to the Shawanese Reserve, Two miles at Kettle Point Lake Huron, two miles square at the River au Sable and two miles square at Bear's Creek also a Reserve for Tomago and his band up the Thames which he will point out when he arrives."

We also asked that the government augment these reserves if "our Great Father's representatives see that they are insufficient for the whole of our Nation now living on this side of the water, to plant corn and hunt, so that we may not be poor and miserable like our Brethren on the American side, who have sold all their Lands & have not made sufficient Reserves for their men, women and children to plant corn." Also to be furnished near each reserve was a blacksmith and husbandman to look after our needs. Both Little Thunder and Red Sky[90] attended this council.

In this original council the government stated that it wanted to buy all the lands north of the Thames River including the River Au Sauble and produced a sketch, which showed the northern boundary of the proposed purchase to be a few miles north of the Au Sable. It was believed to contain 712,000 acres. There was a second council in the late winter of 1819 in which we were told that the government wanted to purchase the lands in two separate treaties. One became known as the Longwoods Tract, which was located on the north shore of the Thames and

---

[90] Written as Mestuckmaybig. See Mesquahwegezhigk/Red Sky in Curnoe, *Deeds/Nations*, 67.

the other became known as the Huron Tract, which was the balance of the land stipulated at the 1818 council.

On March 30, 1819 a provisional agreement was signed for the Huron Tract but the area to be ceded had increased dramatically from the original 712,000 acres to 2.8 million acres. A perpetual annuity of £1375 was to be paid. However, a provisional treaty was signed July 8, 1825 but the annuity was dropped to £1100. The four reserves comprised a total of 23.054 acres. The confirmatory treaty was signed July 10, 1827 for a surrender of 2.2 million acres with a perpetual annuity of £1100. The aggregate acreage for the four reserves was only 17,951 acres.

We were never paid for the additional land ceded. It was an injustice that "made our hearts and feelings so troubled" for decades. In a quest for justice our council appealed to Queen Adelaide, the wife of William VI, by way of an address signed January 6, 1841 and delivered to her in England by Chief David Wawanosh.[91] In it we laid out our claim that we "were prevailed upon a long time ago to sell…a very large…tract of country commencing on the south side of the river Au Sable" and that "when Colonel Givins came again, he said…our Great Father wants a piece of land to make the line straight, so as to run northwest of all the banks of the Au Sable…For this additional piece of land Colonel Givins fixed no price, but said he could not tell how much our Great Father would give us for the same, being ten miles beyond Goderich, and forty miles more north than Colonel Givens ever bought… and has never since paid us." Depending on the "maguanimity, justice and honor of our Great Father to remunerate us for this additional land" we signed Provisional Treaty 27½ and Confirmatory Treaty 29

---

[91] *Address of Port Sarnia Indiands*, MPHSC, Vol. 12, 455-457.

ceding the supplementary tract. Our supplication for justice from the British Crown fell on deaf ears and to this day the issue remains unresolved.

In May of 1820 a provisional treaty was signed for the Longwoods Tract and a sketch was included showing two reserves, one for Tomago and his band on the Thames and one for Kitchemughqua and his band at the headwaters of Big Bear Creek. The confirmatory treaty, signed July 8, 1822, contained provision for a reserve "situate on the northerly side of the River Thames...containing fifteen thousand three hundred and sixty acres. Also reserving two miles square...near the source of Big Bear Creek".[92]   The Big Bear Creek reserve never materialized.

The treaty making process covered nine years and multiple agreements. The subtle changes in these various agreements produced profound consequences. The northern point on Lake Huron had changed from a few miles north of the Au Sable River to a few miles north of the Maitland River (see Appendix 1) adding hundreds of thousands of acres to the surrender. The Huron Tract lost 25% of the promised reserved lands and the Longwoods Tract lost a reserve altogether. The annuity for the Huron Tract was reduced by £275. No provision for expansion of reserved lands if needed was confirmed and no blacksmiths or agricultural instructors were provided. At the beginning of the process we left the valuation entirely up to "our Great Father's representative" expecting fair and just treatment. It appears that we didn't get it.

Little Thunder was still active and well able to travel at his advanced age. He travelled by canoe to Amherstburg in April of 1825 to sign Provisional Treaty No. 27½ for the surrender of

---

[92] Indian Treaties, Treaty No. 280½ Vol. 2, 281.

parts of the Western and London Districts of Upper Canada. He made the journey again in July 1827 to sign Confirmatory Treaty No. 29. It can also be seen by the council minutes of 1818 our chiefs considered Sombra Township (the Shawanese Reserve) to be a reserve for our use named after our Shawanee brothers from Ohio.

During the first two decades of the life of the Upper St. Clair Reserve there had been complaints against Wawanosh for his overbearing and dictatorial methods of leadership. On August 12, 1838 several Chiefs and Principal Men presented a petition to the Lieutenant Governor of Upper Canada asking that Wawanosh be removed as Head Chief. It stated "he had been usurping the rights and privileges of Head Chief over us acting a most dishonest part by robbing us of our goods and money."[93] On September 26, 1838 five chiefs, in a letter of complaint to Wm. Jones, Resident Superintendent of Indian Affairs in the Sarnia area, referred to Wawanosh as "that great rogue and liar".[94] In 1841 Wawanosh was under fire from the Band at Walpole Island who had drawn up a petition of complaint against him.

In 1839, Malcolm Cameron, a wealthy land speculator and politician, approached the Chief Superintendent of Indian Affairs, Samuel Peter Jarvis, with a plan to purchase a tract of land one mile wide by four miles long from off the back end of the Upper St. Clair Reserve. He claimed to have negotiated with three chiefs. Cameron followed this up by writing to Jarvis on November 9, 1839 informing him that he had conferred with Head Chief Wawanosh and had struck a bargain with us to

---

[93] Court File No. 95-CU-92484, 1995. Ontario Court (General Division) between The Chippewas of Sarnia Band and Attorney General of Canada, et al., 22.
[94] Ibid.

purchase four square miles of our reserve. In less than a week Jarvis advised that a formal surrender to the Crown was required as per the Proclamation of 1763 and other laws in effect at the time.

The terms of the deal was never given us by any Crown representative nor was there ever any public meeting held to explain the transaction. There was never any vote taken by the general membership of the Band nor did any of our chiefs or principal men of our community fix their marks on any documents witnessed by any Crown officials.

Notwithstanding any of these requirements in 1840 the Executive Council of the Province of Upper Canada issued an Order-in-Council approving the proposed sale to Cameron. On August 13, 1853, the Province of Canada issued Letters Patent to Cameron for 2,540 acres of our land. Both Jones and Jarvis had fiduciary duties invested in them by the Crown and were responsible for our protection. They both failed in their duties.

In 1842 the Governor General of the Province of Canada, Sir Charles Bagot, appoint a commission to look into irregularities and improprieties being committed in the Indian Department. It was found that neither the Commissioner of Crown Lands nor the Chief Superintendent kept proper accounts of Indian land sales including the one to Cameron. No record keeping of any monies received was kept either by Jarvis or Jones. The down payment made by Cameron was deposited into Jarvis' personal bank account and the money trail ends there.

Both Jarvis and Jones were removed from office as a result of the Bagot Commission. Wawanosh underwent a formal inquiry into his conduct and was dismissed as Head Chief by the Governor General. However, our lands were never returned.

With practice we would get better at negotiating, however it would cost us in terms of land ownership. Over the next century our reserve was reduced in size to approximately 3,100 acres. In the 1970s we negotiated with the Province for a cessation of land to be used for a highway extension. On the south side of the reserve the Province expropriated the land it required from white farmers at $300 an acre. They were forced to pay up to ten times that amount for reserve land because expropriation was not an option. This caused Chief Aylmer Plain to comment "Gradually our Indian people have learned to be vocal and determined to retain the few rights they still have, taking a lesson from every land transaction...until, to-day, the Chippewas of Sarnia will dare to match wits with the sharpest of negotiators".[95]

---

[95] Aylmer N. Plain, *History of the Sarnia Indian Reserve* (Brights Grove, ON: G. Smith, 1975), 16 quoted in Schmalz, *Ojibwa*, 212.

11

19th Century Recollections

The first judge to enter St. Clair County, Michigan Territory, was the Hon. Zephaniah W. Bunce. He arrived from Detroit in 1817 and became good friends with Little Thunder. "Judge Bunce states that when he came to the county, this Indian was one hundred and five years old, five and a half feet high, energetic and capable of attending to his corn-field, four miles south of Black River, as well as to the chase [hunt]. Every New Year's Day, he was accustomed to sail down the river in his large birchen canoe, on the bow of which he would fling the American colors to the breeze. On such an occasion, he would don his gold laced coat, beaded moccasins and leggings, and all the ornaments in his possession."[96]

Within a year of his death in 1827 Little Thunder walked

---

[96] *History of St. Clair County*, A.T. Andreas, 608.

several miles to visit Judge Bunce proudly wearing his English uniform. He was buried wearing that same Brigadier General's jacket and his King George the Third medal in the same mound as his father, Young Gull. Great numbers of our people assembled to honour his memory. Little Thunder had two sons, Red Sky and Anchau, as well as three daughters, one of which married Chief Ogotig. She was well known in this area as Mrs. Ogotig and died on the Upper St. Clair Reserve in 1882 at the age of 107. Little Thunder's brother, Shignebeck, lived to 109 years of age and a third brother, Onsha is also said to have lived to a very old age.

Red Sky had one son; Ozahshkedawa or Nicholas Plain Sr. Nicholas was married three times first to Annie and they had two children Peter and Mary. He then married one of Chief Cheebican's daughters named Betsy and had one son James. Cheebican was a signatory of the 1827 Treaty as was Quaikeegon the father of his third wife, Jemima. Quaikeegon was baptized Jacob and his daughter's name was Jemima Jacob. Ozahshkedawa had five children from this union, Levi, Nicholas Jr., Susanna, Amos and Lucy. Only the first three survived to adulthood.

James attended the Manual Training School at Muncey Town and learned the trade of carpentry. Upon graduation he received a diploma and a chest full of tools. When he returned to Aamjiwnaang he was awarded a contract to make coffins for the community, for which the band paid fifteen dollars each.

Naykeezhig or Driving Clouds, a grandson of the old civil chief Mashkeash, and nephew of Little Thunder was one of the signatories of the treaty of 1836 in Washington, D.C. ceding the Swan Creek and Black River reserves. The terms of the treaty provided cash, goods and land west of the Mississippi. Naykeezhig's cousin, Keewaygeezhig the son of Mrs. Ogotig, also signed this treaty. Most of the Swan-Creek/Black-River bands including Naykeezhig and Keewaygezhig's families joined our brothers at Saginaw.

Shignebeck had a niece who married Alexander Rodd. This was the same man shot and killed by Wawanosh in 1812. She became known as Old Mother Rodd and was quite well known in the area in the nineteenth century. With an abundance of character she had many friends on both sides of the river, but was particularly fond of Americans. She often paddled her canoe from Sarnia to Port Huron as well as downriver to Walpole Island. Old Mother Rodd once met a squirrel swimming in the river and she whacked it with her paddle. She explained that she thought it was a British squirrel and she didn't want it to land on the American side. She lived on the Upper St. Clair Reserve but for many decades sold her crafts (brooms, baskets and mats) in Port Huron.

She was also quite well versed in herbs and medicines and was adept at the craft of healing. One day Wahngohezheget, a son of Mrs. Ogotig, went to Mother Rodd because he had fallen in love with a young woman but he already had a wife. She treated him for wanting to leave his wife by preparing a sweat lodge. The treatment is said to have worked because he remained with his wife until his death.

Old Mother Rodd's portrait hung in the State Library at Lansing. She died on the Upper St. Clair Reserve in 1870 at an age variously reported to be from 104 to 117. Two of her children, Antoine Rodd and Mrs. Charlotte Dupre were also residents of Aamjiwnaang.

Okemos, the brave Ahnishenahbek chief from Cedar River, on the western edge of Aamjiwnaang territory and who fell severely wounded at Sandusky, became well known throughout South-eastern Michigan. He was born on an island in a lake near Pontiac, Michigan but lived on the Cedar River. Although he had pledged allegiance to the Americans he still collected his annuity from the British for service in the War of 1812.

On one occasion in 1844 he stopped to visit at Port Huron while on his way to collect his war veteran's annuity at Sarnia. He had his wife with him who was so sick with consumption that he had to carry her to their canoe. As he reached the mid point of the St. Clair River he hoisted the Union Jack, but to no avail. He was denied his payment. His fortunes continued to sour. His wife died while there so he returned to the Riley settlement where he buried her. He died on the Looking Glass River just east of De Witt, Michigan in 1858 at the age of one hundred. A monument to his honour stands tall at the present city of Okemos, Michigan, which is named after him.

There were four traditional cemeteries in Aamjiwnaang, three on the west side of the river and one on the east side. The one on the east side was located about a half-mile south of the mouth of Mission Creek, which was located at the foot of Confederation Street in present day Sarnia. One was located on the north side of the Pine River at its mouth (present day St. Clair, MI.). Another was located on the south side of the Black River at the present site of Customs Pl. at the foot of Sixth Street in downtown Port Huron. When the U.S. Customs House was about to be built on this site some friends of the Ahnishenahbek moved our forefather's remains to a new site south of the city. There was a fourth cemetery located on the banks of the St. Clair (at the foot of Griswold Avenue, present day Port Huron).

Another signatory of the Treaty of Detroit was a chief by the name of Puckenas or Spark of Fire. He originally "emigrated from a band of Indians located at Georgian Bay, Lake Superior, many years ago, and remained with the Sarnia

Band one summer and one winter, and then returned to home at Georgian Bay. Soon after his arrival home he killed a number of his band, fled from justice and came back to Sarnia. And there represented himself to be a Metahbick [Petahdick family?][97] Indian, and asked to be admitted temporarily into our band, and was admitted, and a tract of land lying east of Sarnia, on a small lake called Wawanosh Lake was allotted him."[98] Puckenas had eleven children. That small lake was named after one of his sons, Wawanosh.

Early in 1816 some Frenchmen who were ice fishing on the Sarnia Bay told Wawanosh that British agents from the Indian Department would be coming to Aamjiwnaang to negotiate a land surrender treaty and that if he told them he was the chief they would record that in their record books. Wawanosh plied the chiefs with an abundant supply of liquor and they agreed to have him be the spokesman for the band. They reasoned he would be best suited for this position because he spoke English fairly well. When the British agents from the Indian Department arrived in the area he told them he was the head chief and was so registered by Indian Affairs. This was how Wawanosh became Head Chief of Aamjiwnaang.

---

[97] Petahdick, Aamjiwnaang Chief, signed Treaties 27½ & 29 with an oak totem, as did Puckenas and Wawanosh.
[98] *Memorial of the Chippewa Indians of Port Sarnia, Walpole Island, Kettle Point and Sauble* (London: s.n., 1871), 2 available from http://www.canadiana.org/eco/english/index.html last accessed 12 June 2006.

12

Prisoners in Our Own Country

On the morning of August 2, 1829 the residents of Aamjiwnaang spotted two canoes ladened with supplies entering the river from Lake Huron. They glided past Fort Gratiot, which was an impressive looking stockade on the American side standing twenty feet above the narrowest part of the river guarding it with one cannon. The canoeists approached our village, which stood at present day downtown Sarnia, and asked to see chief Wawanosh. They were invited into the chief's house, which was the only log home on the reserve. The leader of the group was introduced.

Kahkewaquonaby or Sacred Feathers was a Mississauga from the Credit River and was serving the British Wesleyan Methodists as a missionary. He would become better know as the Reverend Peter Jones. He asked Wawanosh if he might present his message to us and was given permission. Later that day he moved to a clearing in the forest where he held a

Methodist style camp meeting. We all listened politely to the Christian message, but none received it.

Sacred Feathers then moved downriver to Walpole Island where he had even less success delivering the "gospel". There he had to contend with head chief Pazhekezhikquashkum or He Who Makes Footsteps in the Sky, a staunch traditionalist. He was an Otahwah born on the Maumee River in Ohio before the American Revolution but lived on the west shore of Lake St. Clair for many years. In the 1820's he moved to Walpole Island where he rose quickly to head chief. He allowed Sacred Feathers to present his message because he was a brother Ahnishenahbi but at the end of his service Pazhekezhikquashkum refused to change his religion. He spoke for himself as well as the Ahnishenahbek at Walpole. He agreed that liquor was ruining the Ahnishenahbek but questioned what kind of people were the white man's religion producing. His reply to Sacred Feathers was, "The white man makes the firewater, he drinks, and sells it to the Indians, he lies and cheats the poor Indian. I have seen him go to his praying-house in Malden, and as soon as he comes out I have seen him go straight to the tavern, get drunk, quarrel, and fight. Now the white man's religion is no better than mine. I will hold fast to the religion of my forefathers, and follow them to the far west."[99]

Kahkewaquonaby returned to the St. Clair Reserve where he stayed for three years but had no conversions. During that time he also visited the old chief at Walpole three or four times but

---

[99] Rev. Peter Jones, *History of the Ojebway Indians; With Especial Reference to Their Conversion to Christianity* (London: A.W. Bennett, 1861), 229-230 available from http://www.canadiana.org/ECO/ItemRecord/35737?id=b0fa8e3c6abfb 66d last accessed 6 July 2006.

Sacred Feathers could not convince him to change his religion. During this time Aamjiwnaang fell into a deplorable condition. Our population was ravaged by wars and disease (small pox and cholera epidemics). At the signing of the 1827 treaty we were enumerated at only four hundred and forty. Our treaty had provision in it for decreasing our annuity as population decreased, but there was no such provision for increases. Even our own authors considered us a "vanishing race".[100]

Our hunting grounds were being ruined. We were expected to stay on our reserves and take up farming. The dominant culture was overwhelming and we were suffering from severe culture shock. We found such a profound change very difficult. According to evidence given to the Colonial Government by Rev. W. Scott, our missionary in 1841, "...the propensity to roving and hunting is almost incredible in respect to the older Indians, and the younger ones are led to follow their example."[101] Many, in fact most, tried to find solace in alcohol. Scott also reported, "They were previously, according to the testimony of all who knew them, in a very wretched and miserable condition, wicked, drunken, and licentious."[102]

In 1832, during this distressing time, the Methodist Mission officially commenced on our reserve. This is commemorated by a monument still located at the foot of Divine Street, which reads, "On this property stood the British Wesleyan Mission to

---

[100] For two examples see Warren, *History*, 72, Jones, *History*, 254-255.

[101] Evidence of Rev. W. Scott (respecting the Indians of the Upper St. Clair Reserve) Reported in 1847, Appendix T, Journals of Legislative Assembly of the Province of Canada, T-167 available from http://www.canadiana.org/ECO/ItemRecord/9_00955_6_1?id=b0fa8e3 c6abfb66d last accessed 6 July 2006.

[102] Ibid.

the Chippewas Indians, Rev. Thom. Turner 1832-34, Rev. James Evans 1834-1838. Erected by the United Church of Canada, Sarnia, 1932". The stone for this monument came from Lot 7, on the River Range of our reserve.

The first convert to be baptized was Old Salt, the same warrior that was with Wawanosh when they were clearing the area of American sympathizers in 1812. He was given the Christian name Peter keeping Salt as his surname. His old companion Wawanosh, who was given the Christian name of Joshua, joined him. The highly respected shaman Chewetagum followed them in late 1834. Once these leaders embraced Christianity the majority followed over the next two years. The community near Sarnia slowly began to recover, but our American brothers were not so fortunate.

The 1830's and 1840's saw a huge influx of refugees, mostly Potawatomi from the United States. Two reasons caused this great migration into Upper Canada. The United States' removal policy was under full implementation. Under this policy the government attempted to force a removal of all First Nations peoples from Indiana, Michigan, Wisconsin and Minnesota territories by a series of cession treaties by which we were to cede all of our land holdings in these territories to the United States of America in a sort of trade for reserves of land west of the Mississippi. Our lands here were to be put up for sale, the monies to be held in trust with all expenses related to our removal deducted from the proceeds. Also the British Colonial government was about to enact a residency clause into their present giving policy.

A Council was held August 20th 1839 at Notawassippi, St. Joseph County, Michigan between the Potawatomi nation and the United States government. According to the Treaty of Fort Armstrong, which ended the Black Hawk war, the Potawatomi were to "give up peaceable possession of the lands ceded to the government of the United States ... and remove west of the Mississippi river".[103]   Chief Muckmote was adamant.   "Father: We have held our consultation with the three nations, and what you said to us yesterday does not please us at all. You told us we must go west of the Mississippi. In our former councils we always said we would not go, and our minds have not changed yet. At the council at Niles the same question was put to us and we said we would not go. We say again, we will not go." After more dialogue another Chief, Red Bird, concluded the council by saying "Father, you have heard our decision: we shall never go ... we will never meet in council again."[104]

Meanwhile the American government relentlessly complained to the British about the handing out of presents to "American Indians" at Manitoulin and Walpole Islands. They felt it only aggravated animosities toward the U.S. government while at the same time it reinforced positive sentiments toward the British in Upper Canada. This was a practice that had gone on for decades, the presents representing recognition of services rendered as British allies through the War of 1812. The presents were being kept up to buy native support in case of more trouble with the United States. Many Potawatomi came from Michigan, Indiana and Wisconsin to receive these payments.

The British colonial government yielded to American complaints in the late 1830s and included a residency clause to their policy on present giving. The "visiting Indians" would no longer be eligible to receive government presents. They then renewed their longstanding invitation to their former allies to

---

[103] "Indian Council" from the White Pigeon Republican, Aug. 28, 1839 reprinted in MPHSC, vol. 10, 170.
[104] Ibid.,172.

immigrate to Upper Canada, especially to the Saugeen Tract.[105]

Thousands of new immigrants flooded into the country. One estimate of the number of Potawatomi arriving from Michigan, Indiana and Wisconsin between 1837 and 1849 was up to 3,000.[106] They crossed the border at Windsor and Sarnia in the south with many settling on Walpole Island. In one crossing alone three hundred Potawatomi refugees entered at Aamjiwnaang in July 1837. They were not totally welcomed here although a few families stayed. They moved north with a few more staying at Kettle and Stoney Points, but the majority moved further north into the Saugeen tract. Many more Potawatomi arrived at Manitoulin Island in the North. However, Manitoulin only served as an entry point with the majority moving south into Saugeen territory looking for more fertile land.

A second immigration affected Aamjiwnaang. After the American treaty of 1836 ceding the Black River and Swan Creek reservations their band members were to remove themselves to new lands west of the Mississippi River. Three of their four chiefs, Naykeezhig, Mayzin and Keewaykeezhig chose to move to Canada with their followers settling at Aamjiwnaang and Bkejwanong. The other chief, Eshtonaquet or Francis Maconce, chose to move to a reservation in Kansas, near present day Ottawa, taking several families with him. In 1859 they agreed to share a reduced reserve with a group of displaced Munsee Delawares. This reserve became known as the Chippewa and Christian Indian Reservation.

---

[105] Stephanie McMullen, *Disunity and Dispossession: Nawash Ojibwa and Potawatomi of the Saugeen Territory, 1836-1865* (M.A. Thesis, University of Calgary, 1997), 37.

[106] Edward S. Rogers and Donald B. Smith, eds., *Aboriginal Ontario* (Toronto: Dundurn Press, 1994), 123.

In 1837 the Saginaw First Nation followed suit ceding all of their holdings as well. This was accomplished under much duress and even though their lands had been taken from them they still refused to go. Now they had become the squatters on American land. This remained the situation until the treaty of 1864, which finally allocated reservation lands for the Saginaw First Nation in Isabella County. The Swan Creek/Black River First Nation received no reservation because in 1855 the "tribal organization" was "dissolved" and the Swan Creek/Black River band remaining in Michigan lost its federal recognition, which they are trying to regain through U.S. Congress Committee hearings today.

Shortly after the War of 1812 the British had presented an invitation for past service to "American Indians" to move to Upper Canada in order to avoid American persecution. As participants in this longstanding invitation we sent wampums in 1837 to Saginaw. These wampums invited any of them who wished to take advantage of the British invitation to become part of our band and participate in the ownership of our lands and in our annuities. A few hundred accepted our offer with most removing themselves to Aamjiwnaang. This was confirmed by a special Act of Council and a tract of land from off the south end of our reserve one half mile wide and four miles deep was allotted to them. Ozahshkedawa at the young age of eighteen was a member of this council.

In 1870 a schism broke out in Aamjiwnaang over the "Saginaw Indians". Joshua Wawanosh, along with Wm. N. Fisher, Interpreter at Walpole Island and seven other followers petitioned, Joseph Howe, Superintendent General of Indian Affairs, to have them removed from the Band list of the Sarnia Reserve and their portion of the annuity disallowed. They basically argued that the "foreign Indians" were only allowed to settle on the Sarnia Reserve temporarily, that they had possessions with improvements thereon in Michigan granted to them under American treaties and that they were never granted Band membership or a share in the annuity by any act of council.[107]

A Memorial in favour of the Saginaw Indians to remain as part of the Band at Sarnia and to retain their share in the annuity countered this. Traditional Head Chief Nicholas Plain, Ozahshkedawa, and grandson of Little Thunder headed this Memorial. Traditional chief Naykeezhig, grandson of Mashkeash, also signed it. This was the same Naykeezhig that was forced to move to Canada by the American 1836 treaty. Also signing this Memorial were traditional chiefs Thomas Nayahnequod and William Isaac, grandsons of Chief Negig, James Meshebezhe, descendent of Chief Meshebezhe, Jacob Petahdick, descendant of Chief Petahdick, Thomas, James and John Johnson, descendents of Chief Wapagance and William Jacob, descendent of Chief Quaikeegon. Over fifty councillors from the Sarnia, Walpole, Kettle Point and Sauble bands also signed it. It essentially stated that the Saginaw Indians were invited to become permanent band members of the Sarnia band, were given two square miles of land to settle on and a permanent share of the annuity by a special Act of Council in 1837. Sworn oaths characterized Wawanosh as a troublemaker

---

[107] *The Memorial of the Chippewa Tribe of Indians, Some of whom reside on their reserve near Sarnia, and others on Walpole Island, together with other documents, praying that they man be allowed to form themselves into one tribe as they were prior to 1831, and to hold their lands and moneys in common, and that the Foreign Indians may be hereafter excluded from participating in the Annuity* (Sarnia: Canadian Power Press Print, 1871) available from http://www.canadiana.org/ECO/ItemRecord/23703?id=7f78ef9eb6812 113 last accessed 20 July 2006.

and Wm. N. Fisher as a drunk. The Saginaw Indians remained and have long since been incorporated into our band.[108]

The assimilation policy in Canada would be taken up in earnest when the responsibility for Indian affairs was transferred to the government of Upper Canada in 1860. This policy remained official government policy for over one hundred years. The cornerstone of this process would be the residential school. These would come under the jurisdiction of the federal government, but the responsibility of day-to-day operations would lay with the Church. Numerous manual labour schools were founded between 1842 and 1878.[109]

The complicity of the Church with the policy of total cultural replacement can be seen in a letter from the Rev. Alexander Sutherland, general secretary of the Methodist Church of Canada, Missionary Department, to Laurence Vankoughnet, deputy superintendent general of Indian affairs: "Experience convinces us that the only way in which the Indian of the country can be permanently elevated and thoroughly civilized is by removing the children from the surroundings of Indian home life, and keeping them separated long enough to form those habits of order, industry, and systematic effort, which they will never learn at home".[110]

Edward Francis Wilson established the Shingwauk residential school for boys at Sault Ste. Marie, Ontario, in 1873.

---

[108] *Memorial of the Chippeway Indians of Port Sarnia, Warpole Island, Kettle Point, and Sauble, touching their claim of the grant of 1,100 currency perpetual annuity: to His Excellency the Governor General in council that the foreign Indians may participate in the annuity* (London, Ont.? : s.n., 1871?) available from http://www.canadiana.org/ECO/ItemRecord/09869?id=7f78ef9eb6812113 last accessed 20 July 2006.

[109]Schmalz, *Ojibwa*, 181-184.

[110]Ibid.,181.

Wilson was an Anglican missionary sent to Canada by the English Church Missionary Society. He was the school's first principal and remained in that post until 1893. All residential schools had the aim of providing the environment for as total a cultural replacement as possible, and Shingwauk was no exception.

Language was seen as a major key in the cultural replacement program. We were not allowed to speak our language during school, chores or play. In order to enforce the ban we were rewarded for checking up on each other. This meant reporting any infractions to Wilson. When this failed, corporal punishment was meted out during the punishment period at seven in the evening. This policy against speaking our own language remained in effect until 1971.

Prohibition against all other forms of culture was also included in the residential schools' rules. At play, we were not allowed to play any First Nations games but were made to play European ones; games such as marbles, cricket and soccer. First Nations forms of music were also forbidden. Shingwauk, like other residential schools, formed a marching band where the boys learned to play European marches and hymns. Other European cultural forms were forced upon us, such as the celebration of western holidays like Christmas, Easter and Dominion Day. Of course, participation in any First Nations feasts or religious ceremonies was strictly forbidden. These assimilationist policies continued well into the twentieth century.[111]

In June 1870 Chief Nicholas Plain Sr. along with William

---

[111]For an excellent exposé on E.F. Wilson and his days as principal of the Shingwauk residential school see David A. Nock, *A Victorian Missionary and Canadian Indian Policy* (Waterloo: Wilfred Laurier University. 1988), 67-100.

Wawanosh, Jonas Henry and John Sumner were invited to attend a General Council of the Six Nations. William Wawanosh was elected to be our delegation's spokesman. The purpose of the council, which also included delegates from different bands across the Province, was to deliberate on a new piece of legislation assented to by parliament in 1869. This legislation would become the infamous Indian Act of 1876. At the General Council Wawanosh seconded a motion "that provision be made by the Dominion Government to allow four natives in the House of Commons, in Ottawa, to represent the different tribes."[112]   The motion was first carried, then reconsidered, then withdrawn.   Chief Nicholas Plain Sr.'s grandson would echo this idea a century later. Overall motions were passed roundly rejecting the new Act.

All this was to no avail. The new Act would become the single most influential object used by the government of Canada to control our lives. Its control was dictatorial and its influence suffocating. "As a deputy minister of the Indian Affairs Branch noted: 'The Indian Act is a Land Act. It is a Municipal Act, an Education Act and a Societies Act. It is primarily social legislation, but has a very broad scope; there is provisions about liquor, agriculture and mining as well as Indian lands, band membership and so forth. It has elements that are embodied in perhaps two dozen different acts of any of the provinces and overrides some federal legislation in some respects . . . It has the force of the Criminal Code and the impact of a constitution on those people and communities that come within its purview.'"[113]

---

[112] "Minutes of the General Council of the Six Nations, and Delegates of Different Bands in Western and Eastern Canada" (Hamilton: Spectator Offices, 1870), 21, 23, 26.
[113] Schmalz, *Ojibway*, 196 quoting Franz M. Koennecke, "Wasoksing: The History of Parry Island, an Anishnabwe Community in the Georgian Bay,

One amendment to the Act in 1884 "imposed two to six month's imprisonment on anyone participating in certain Indian religious acts".[114] It was amended again in 1889 to allow "greater federal government control over Indian education, morality, local government and land. For example, our most valued possession, our land, could be taken without our consent for leasing to non-Indians".[115]

Enfranchisement was the most discriminatory section. It allowed a First Nations man to gain all the rights and privileges of Canadians, including citizenship and the right to vote and hold office, if he were to allow the registrar to remove his name from the Indian Register. He lost his birthright, including treaty rights and band rights, which also included the right to live and hold land on his reserve. In effect, he became a white man in everything but colour. This section was forced on First Nations women when they married a non-First Nations man. "In 1880 an amendment declared that any Indian with a university degree would ipso facto be enfranchised and therefore no longer be an Indian under the act".[116] This also enforced enfranchisement on First Nations people who gained a profession or became ordained. Although enfranchisement was finally repealed in 1984 some sub-sections were repealed earlier.[117]

The practice of patronage appointments was the mechanism used to enforce the Indian Act. Bureaucrats called Indian Agents were appointed to serve on reserves in order to enforce

---

1850-1920" (MA Thesis, University of Waterloo, 1984), 263.
[114]Schmalz, *Ojibwa*, 205.
[115]Ibid.,207.
[116]Ibid.,198.
[117]For a good overview of the 1857 Enfranchisement Act see Rogers and Smith, eds., *Aboriginal Ontario*, 199-201 and for the 1885 Franchisement Act, 235-239.

the act locally on our assets and us.[118]

Indian Agents had such absolute power over the life of First Nations communities that the people viewed the government as a dictatorship. The Church was also viewed as a part of that dictatorship because, to a certain extent, the local minister or priest shared in the power imposed on us. Basil Johnston of Cape Croker, poignantly describes his 1939 childhood experience of being sent to the residential school at Spanish, Ontario:

> The reason for and the mode of my own committal were typical. My parents had separated, and, following the break-up, Mother, my four sisters and I lived with my grandmother for a while.

> But unknown to either my mother or my grandmother, the Indian agent and the priest has conferred – with nothing but our welfare in mind, of course – and decided that not even the combined efforts of Grandmother and Mother were enough to look after five children and that they ought to be relieved of two of their burdens . . .

> On the fateful day, Grandmother and Mother wept as they scrubbed and polished and clothed me in the finest second-hand clothing that they had been able to scrounge at the bazaar . . .

> Mr. F. Tuffnel did not come in as invited; instead he stood at the doorway, glowering through his rimless glasses and pursing his mouth as if afraid to open it

---

[118]Schmalz, *Ojibwa*, 212.

lest he be contaminated.

Mr. Tuffnel unstitched his lips after looking at me and rasped, 'Well! Where's the other one?'

'She's sick,' Mother replied in her best English. 'Got poison ivy, her . . . in bed.' . . .

The agent flinched perhaps not wanting to catch poison ivy. 'Well, gotta take two at least,' he said . . . 'How about her?' he rasped, pointing at . . . my four year old sister.

Mother and Grandmother were both appalled. 'No! She's too young,' they wailed. 'She can't go to school yet, she's only four. No!'

But the agent knew how to handle Indians, especially Indian women. 'Well, if you don't want her to go, we'll take the whole family. Now! Get her ready. Hurry up!'

Mother and Grandmother whimpered as they washed and clothed my sister.[119]

Indeed, the Indian agent had sweeping powers, powers far greater than any chief had under traditional government. Nothing came into the community or left the community without his approval. No band resolution was valid unless he passed them onto the Department of Indian Affairs for their approval. In fact, no band council meeting had any power unless he was present. Their duties involved corresponding

---

[119]Basil H. Johnston, *Indian School Days* (Toronto: Key Porter Books, 1988), 19-20.

with the federal government on every circumstance. He was the sole purchasing agent for the community, buying all the cattle, seed and farm implements. He was also the sole selling agent, responsible for selling the farm produce. He managed the community's bank accounts. He tendered and oversaw all building construction. He also acted as judge in civil disputes and was the inspector of education in the community.[120] Unfortunately, because of the system of patronage appointments, very rarely were Indian agents of the quality essential to undertake such responsibilities. Consequently, our communities suffered greatly.

I do not intend to paint a picture of total corruption and abuse. There were some good Indian agents. There were also many good missionaries, ministers and priests. Many of these spoke out against the oppressive domination of the prevalent society, but they were visionaries far ahead of their time and notably in the minority.

One such figure was Froome Talfourd. He took over the visiting superintendency at St. Clair in 1858. Upon doing so, he found that we had lodged numerous complaints about missing moneys from land transactions and late payments from such large corporations as the Grand Western Railway Company. He investigated and found the discrepancies in the Land Account Books indicated that embezzlement was involved. He reported this to Lord Bury, the superintendent general of Indian affairs.[121]

This was one of many incidents in which Talfourd stood up on the side of his First Nations charge. So fair, honest and upright was he in his dealings with the St. Clair Reserve that he quickly gained a highly regarded reputation among us, so much

---

[120]Schmalz, *Ojibway*, 208.
[121]Ibid.,169-170.

so, in fact, that we instituted a feast in his honour. Nicholas Plain Jr. writes in his 1951 short history, "Among the Indians he was known as 'The Englishman who keeps his word.' . . . The Indians of the Sarnia Reserve tendered him a banquet on his birthday, November 4th . . . The Talfourd Feast was one event in the year that no Indian missed. Even the aged and sick had steaming plates of food delivered to their homes."[122]

During the months of March through June 1891, a series of four articles appeared in The Canadian Indian under the pseudonym of "Fair Play".[123] The articles advocated cultural synthesis rather than cultural replacement (forced assimilation). Cultural synthesis is defined as encouraging "the synthesis of two cultures, that retains the elements of both, and that encourages the voluntary borrowing and adaptation by the weaker cultural system . . . the cultural components from different societies will be combined in ways that make sense to the borrowing society".[124]

The articles also advocated a high degree of political autonomy. "He suggests it would constitute no harm or menace to Canada if the Indians of Ontario 'were permitted to have their own centre of Government – their own Ottawa, so to speak; their own Lieutenant-Governor, and their own Parliament'".[125] These few grand ideas of the latter half of the

---

[122]Nicholas Plain, *The History of Chippewas of Sarnia and the History of Sarnia Reserve* (Sarnia, ON: Privately Printed, 1951), 30.

[123]Nock argues that the author of the "Fair Play" articles was E.F. Wilson, despite the fact that the thrust of the articles went against the grain of the policies of the Shingwauk residential school, an institution founded and run for the first twenty years by him. See David A. Nock, *A Victorian Missionary*, 135-150.

[124]Ibid.,1-2.

[125]Ibid.,136 quoting Fair Play, The Future of Our Indians, Paper No. 3, *The Canadian Indian* 1, no. 9 (June 1891), 254.

19th century succumbed to the more dominant paternalism in its many forms, which reached its zenith during this time period, much to our detriment.

After World War II both the government and the public at large began to question Canada's Indian Policy. A joint committee of House Representatives and the Senate was formed to study the matter. As a result the Indian Act of 1876 underwent extensive revision. As a result we regained our right to attend traditional religious ceremonies, to drink alcohol in public places such as bars and taverns, and compulsory enfranchisement ended (except in the case of native women marrying non-native men). The revised Act also gave individual band councils more authority.[126] Assimilation was still the government's official policy but it would now be allowed to happen gradually and would not be forced upon us.

The assimilation policy culminated with Pierre Elliott Trudeau's Liberal Government and its 1969 White Paper. This was the last official blueprint for cultural replacement and assimilation. It proposed to terminate all special rights and separate recognition of First Nations including the Indian Act, reserves and treaties. In return, First Nations people would receive the same legal rights and recognition as other Canadians.[127]

First Nations vehemently opposed the policy. For example, Chief Fred Plain, president of the Union of Ontario Indians at the time, countered the policy by presenting "a brief to Ottawa which would give twelve seats in the House of Commons to Indian representatives . . . He pointed out that New Zealand already had such a plan in effect for its Maori population".[128]

---

[126] Rogers and Smith, *Aboriginal Ontario*, 396.
[127]Ibid.,n18, 9.
[128]Schmalz, *Ojibwa*, 251.

This plan was not adopted, but because of the massive opposition to the White Paper it was formally withdrawn in 1971.

In 1970, Jeannette (Corbière) Lavell of Manitoulin Island registered an injunction prohibiting the registrar from removing her name from the Indian Register because she married a non-First Nations person. She used the Bill of Rights clause against sexual discrimination and won in the lower courts. However, she lost in the Supreme Court. The Indian Act took precedence over the Bill of Rights. On the other hand, Sandra Lovelace of the Tobique Reserve in New Brunswick took her similar case to the United Nations. In 1981 Canada was found in violation of an international covenant on human rights. As a result the Indian Act was rewritten to remove sexual discrimination and married First Nations women and their children were allowed to regain lost status.[129]

Returning to the beginnings of our reserve, Red Sky died sometime between 1819 and 1825 leaving his young son an orphan. He was adopted and raised by an old lady who had her wigwam pitched on the Black River and he came across to the St. Clair Reserve in 1834. As a very young man, about age fourteen, he became disenchanted with reserve life and all of the misery it brought. After hearing the many stories of traditional life in the "old days" he thought if he went west he would find the "land of souls" where he could live among the ancestors in perfect peace and harmony. To this end he travelled by canoe on a journey as far as the foothills of the Rocky Mountains meeting many people of the different Nations along the way. He never found his "promised land" so returned four years later to the accolades of our people. He was invited to sit on the

---

[129] Schmalz, *Ojibwa*. 256-257.

Council and at a special naming ceremony he was given a new name, Ozahshkedawa, or On The Plain.

Ozahshkedawa converted to Christianity and was baptized by the Methodist missionary. It was the practice of the missionaries to give all new adherents to the faith a Christian name. Sometimes they would leave the person's Ahnishenahbek name as a surname or sometimes they would drop the traditional name and replace it with a European surname. Other times they would translate the traditional name into English and that would become the surname. In Ozahshkedawa's case they shortened the English interpretation of his name to Plain and gave him the Christian name of Nicholas. This is why the descendants of Ozahshkedawa are the Plains of Aamjiwnaang.

Appendix 1—Maps

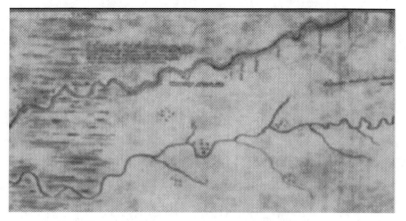

British Naval Surveyors Map—River Thames[130]

---

[130] U.K. Hydrographic Archives, No. 23 1aA, ca. 1815, See Darlene Johnston, *Connecting People to Place: Aboriginal History in Cultural Context* available at http://www.ipperwashinquiry.ca/ last accessed on 14 July 2006.

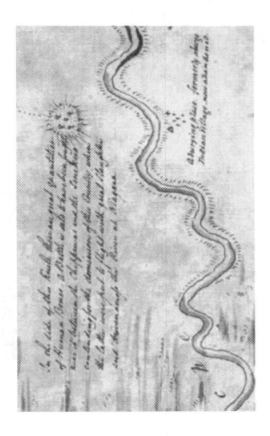

Zoom Image of River Thames Map[131]

---

[131] Location of knoll is twelve miles upstream from the river's mouth. The caption reads, "In the side of this knoll there are great quantities of human bones. A battle is said to have been fought near it between the Chippewas and Senekies contending for the dominion of this country, when the latter were put to flight with great slaughter and driven across the river at Niagara.

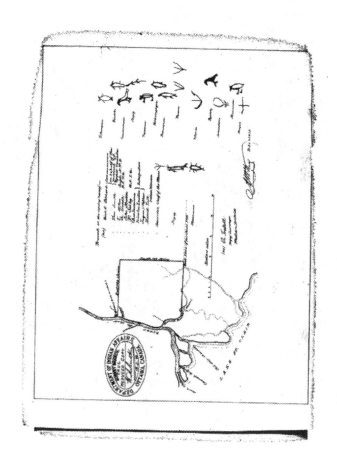

Map from Treaty 7, 1796—NAC

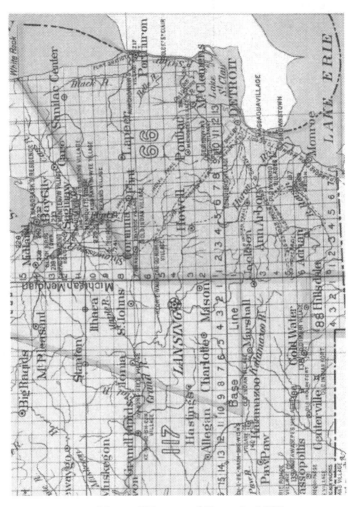

Map of Treaty of Detroit, 1807
Ceding Area 66—LC

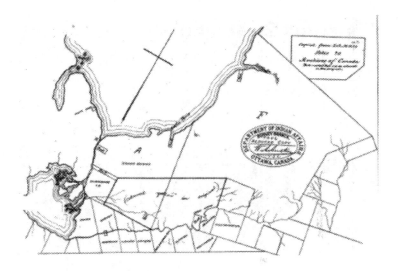

Map of Treaty 21, 1819—NAC

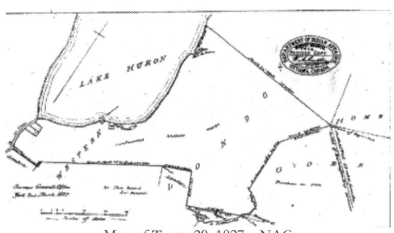

Map of Treaty 29, 1827—NAC

Appendix 2—Treaties

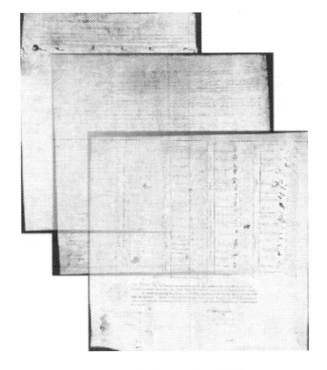

Treaty of Greenville, 1795

Extracts From the Treaty of Greenville, 1795[132]

---

[132] Salutation reads, George Washington President of the United States of America—To All To Whom These Presents Come—Greeting. The signatory Nemekass (Little Thunder) is Animikeence see Curnoe, *Deeds/Nations*, 6.

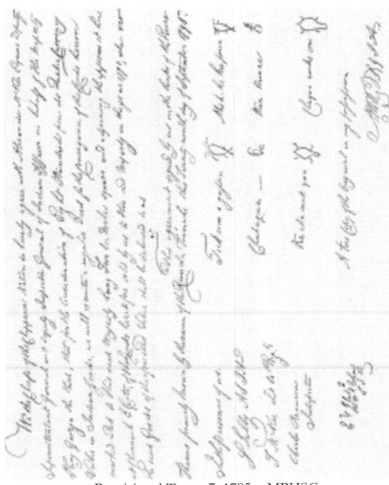

Provisional Treaty 7, 1795—MPHSC

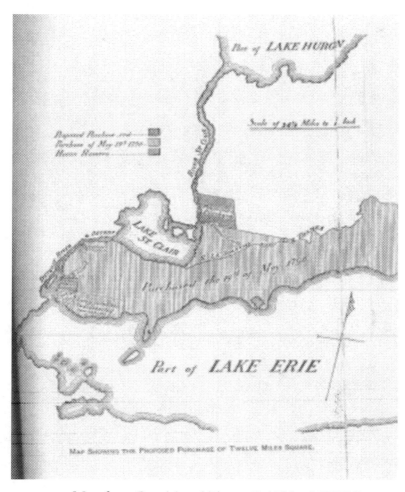

Map from Provisional Treaty 7, 1795—MPHSC

104 .   COLONIAL OFFICE RECORDS.

COL. A. MC KEE TO JOSEPH CHEW.

Extract of a Letter from Alexander McKee Esquire Deputy Supor intendant General &c. to Joseph Chew Esqr, Secretary to the Indian Department, dated Detroit 24th October 1795.

"I am just returned from the River Thames and the Channail Ecarte where I have held Councils with the Chiefs of the Chippewas, and entered into a Provisional Agreement with them for the Pur chase of Twelve miles Square at Channail Ecarte pursuant to His Excellency Lord Dorchester's directions, intended by His Lordship's benevolence for the future residence of such of the Western Nations of Indians as have been driven from their Country by the Army of the United States."

"Their numbers cannot be ascertained at present with any degree of exactness, but I have reason to believe the greatest part of those who have been so long at Swan Creek and also the Ottawas of the River Rasine, will go to these Lands and may amount to between Two and Three Thousand."

"The Chippawas are the only Proprietors of these Lands, and I am happy to state that they most readily consented to a sale thereof and chearfully embraced my proposal; Some of the Chiefs of the Ottawas accompanied me to view the spot which their Fathers good ness had suggested as a convenient situation for them to set down upon, are extremely happy in having soon a country every way proper and calculated as well for Hunting as Cornfields and villages and they express and earnest desire to be permitted to plant thereon as soon as the season will allow them in the Spring."

Enclosed B.
in Lord Dorchester's No. 87 to the Duke of Portland.

[Q 75-2, p 474]

Re: Treaty 7[133]—MPHSC

---

[133] *A. McKee to J. Chew*, MPHSC, Vol. 24, 104.

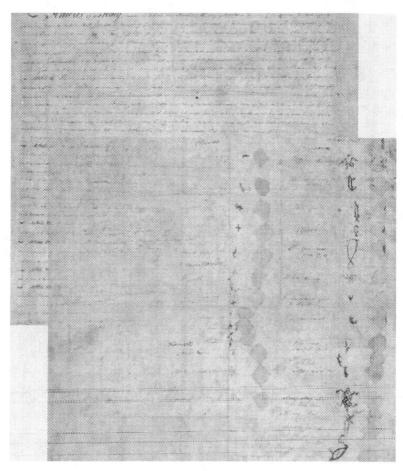

Treaty of Detroit, 1807

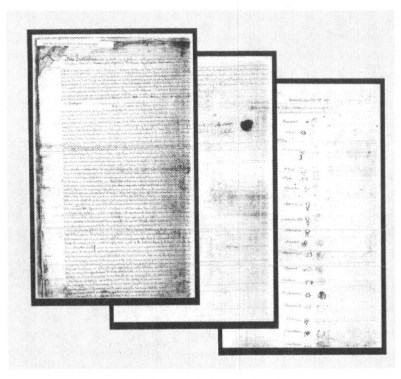

Treaty 29, 1827—NAC

KEY TO ABBREVIATIONS

MPHSC   Michigan Pioneer Historical Society Collection

LC   Library of Congress

NAC   National Archives of Canada

NYCD   New York Colonial Documents

OVGLEA:MC   Ohio Valley-Great Lakes Ethnohistory Archives: Miami Collection

ROM   Royal Ontario Museum

WHS   Wisconsin Historical Society

SELECTED BIBLIOGRAPHY

Blackbird, Andrew J. *History of the Ottawa and Chippewa Indians of Michigan.* Ypsilanti, MI: The Ypsilanti Job Printing House, 1887 available at http://www.canadiana.org/ECO/PageView?id=a31b3e758 e50350b&display=00429+0003 last accessed 27 June 2006.

Copway, G. *The Traditional History and Characteristics of the Ojibway Nation.* London: Charles Gilpin, 1850 available from http://www.canadiana.org/eco/english/index.html last accessed 18 July 2006.

Curnoe, Greg. *Deeds/Nations*, ed. Frank Davey and Neal Farris. London, ON: London Chapter, OAS, Occasional Publication #4, 1996.

Johnston, Basil. *Indian School Days.* Toronto: Key Porter Books Ltd., 1988.

Jones, Rev. Peter. *History of the Ojebway Indians; With Especial Reference to Their Conversion to Christianity.* London: A.W. Bennett, 1861 available from http://www.canadiana.org/ECO/ItemRecord/35737?id=b

0fa8e3c6abfb66d last accessed 6 July 2006.

Kinietz, Vernon W. *The Indians of the Western Great Lakes 1615-1760*. Ann Arbor: University of Michigan Press, 1940; Ann Arbor Paperbacks, Ann Arbor: 1991.

Mahon, John K. *The War of 1812*. New York: Da Cappo Press, 1991.

Parkman, Francis. *Montcalm and Wolfe: The French and Indian War*. New York: Da Cappo Press, 1995.

Plain, Aylmer N. *History of the Sarnia Indian Reserve*. (Brights Grove, ON: G. Smith, 1975), 16 quoted in Schmalz, Ojibwa, 212.

Plain, Nicholas. *The History of Chippewas of Sarnia and the History of Sarnia Reserve*. Sarnia, ON: Privately Printed, 1951.

Rogers Edward S. and Donald B. Smith, ed., *Aboriginal Ontario*. Toronto: Dundurn Press, 1994.

Schmalz, Peter S. *The Ojibwa of Southern Ontario*. Toronto: University of Toronto Press, 1991.

Smith, Donald B. *Sacred Feathers*. Toronto: University of Toronto Press, 1997.

Sugden, John. *Tecumseh: A Life*. New York: Henry Holt and Co., 1997.

Warren, William W. *History of the Ojibway People*. St. Paul: Minnesota Historical Society Press, vol. 5, 1885; Borealis Books, 1984.

INDEX

Index   149